SPEAKING TO THE HEART
FROM FLICKER TO FLAME
VOLUME ONE

MOMENTS BEYOND THE VEIL

Second edition

APRIL YARBER

Speaking to the Heart Publishing © 2021

23052 Alicia Pkwy suite H 132
Mission Viejo Calif, 92692

SPEAKING to the HEART from Flicker to Flame Vol. 1 copyright © 2021 by April Yarber, all rights reserved.

copyright allowance for all contributing writers of this anthology
they may reprint or use their own personal stories in any/all other works at their discretion.

Graphic Book Cover design by Amanda Turney
Edited by April Yarber
Creator, Compiler, Co- Author April Yarber
All Scripture quotations, unless otherwise noted, taken from the HOLY BIBLE: ENGLISH STANDARD VERSION-**ESV** published in 2001 by Crossway, having been "created by a team of more than 100 leading evangelical scholars and pastors." The (*ESV*) is derived from the 1971 *edition* of the Revised *Standard Version* **(RSV)** text.

Scripture quotations designated **(WEB)** World English Bible

Scripture quotations designated (**NIV**) are from the HOLY BIBLE:
NEW INTERNATIONAL VERSION ® Copyright© 1973, 1978, 1984, 2011 by Biblica. All rights reserved worldwide.

Scripture quotations designated (**NLT**) New Living Translation

All rights reserved. No part of this book may be reproduced or transmitted in any form or by any means, electronic or mechanical, including photocopying, recording, or by any information storage and retrieval system, without written permission of the publisher. Unless a contributor in this written work.

Library of Congress Control Number: 2 0 2 1 9 1 9 2 5 0

ISBN: (Second edition Paperback) 978-1-7379673-2-3

ISBN: (first edition Paperback) 978-1-7379673-0-9

ISBN: (e-book) 978-1-7379673-1-6

This book *is* filled with Holy Spirit Power.

I pray a special verse over all the contributors and readers of this book.

In the mighty name of

Jesus

PSALM 91

Amen

DEDICATIONS

*This is a book dedicated to
our Lord Jesus
for whom I write, all for His glory.*

*And to all my family thank you for all your support.
To my contributors God bless your Hearts!*

As always with love, April

ACKNOWLEDGMENTS

I want to thank all the people who contributed their personal stories. Sharing them openly with me about the experiences they have had with our Lord's Presence, and about the times that he has allowed them to glimpse beyond the veil taking their FAITH from FLICKER TO FLAME. These are the moments that keep our hearts on fire. Thank you for opening- up to the world. Sharing your experiences, and showing others how truly awesome, mighty, merciful, forgiving, and loving our Lord Jesus Christ is. It is my honor to be able to hear so many beautiful stories of God's love and the impact he makes on people's lives every day in His own mysterious, miraculous, and perfect ways.

As everything is always His timing…

There is a time for everything,
and a season for every activity under the heavens:

- (Ecclesiastes 3:1, NIV)

INTRODUCTION

This book is based on many peoples true accounts of personal experience's they have had of a spiritual kind. When I read through the stories:

I see a pattern of the Lord showing up in unexpected ways as if to say, *"Look my child I am here. Do not worry, you are not alone. I have been with you all along."*

It is in these beautiful moments that we feel the wholeness and fullness of God. We feel His Presence and that ever so calming closeness to Him, as He pulls back the veil, allowing us to momentarily see and feel with a certainty, not found in this world, that we are not alone- and in these moments, just beyond the veil, we know without a doubt that all things will be ok, because he has allowed us to truly see the power of His hand working in and among the situations of our lives.[1] Working all things together for our good…

---

[1]Romans 8:28 NIV **28** *And we know that in all things God works for the good of those who love him, who[a] have been called according to his purpose.*

Also, we know that at all times, although we *cannot* see him, He *is* here. We know He sends His angels to watch over us, as He gives to us these beautiful leading breadcrumbs, that takes our *Faith* from *Flicker to Flame*, just when we need it the most. We are free to live and move with a refreshed confidence, without the doubts of the world. We are free yes, to bask in the glow and soak ourselves with the awe and wonder of our *Lord* and His marvelous works.

> *For in Him we live and move and have our being; as even some of your own poets have said, "For we are indeed His offspring."*
> *- (Acts 17:28, ESV)*

CONTENTS

The Beginning
ASKING JESUS IN

Page 13

Bill Sterling
THE SEMI-TRUCK INCIDENT

Page 21

Diane Reyes
THE MIRACLE OF DAVID

Page 27

Shirl Thomas
A LIGHT OF PEACE
JESUS- MY COMPANION

Page 49

Mason Zepeda
IN THE ARMS OF AN ANGEL

Page 55

Priscilla James Cruz
THE VISION

Page 61

April Yarber
HE CALLS ME OUT OF THE MUCK
ANOINTED WITH LOVE

Page 67

Colleen Rosencrans
BLUEBIRD ON MY SHOULDER

Page 82

Clay Rosencrans
THE WAY MAKER

Page 86

Jackie Gebbia
HE LIVES
THE WHITE FEATHER
HE HEARS YOU

Page 94

April Yarber-Berg
HIS PERFECT TIME

———

Page 106

Shannon Lumley
GOD'S GOT YOU COVERED

———

Page 109

Monica Ayala
ANGELS STANDING GUARD

———

Page 113

April Yarber-Berg
ANSWERED PRAYERS

———

Page 118

James Berg
FOCUS ON HIM

———

Page 125

Debi Golceker
BEAUTIFUL LILY AT THE BANQUET TABLE

Page 129

Joy Ingram Grabarkewitz
HAVING FAITH

Page 137

Agnes Higginbotham
EARTH ANGEL
THE VISITING ANGEL
THE ANGEL OF COMFORT

Page 144

Nicole Gardner
AWAKENING DESIRE
THE FIRST ASSIGNMENT
THE SINGLE ROSE

Page 151

April Yarber-Berg
IMPENATRABLE PEACE

Page 158

Darlene Harris
OBEDIENT BLESSINGS

Page 167

Denise Thurman
MY DREAM HOME

Page 168

Dr. Keith Broyles
LAKE SILENCE

Page 182

Nolan Welch
AN UNDENIABLE MESSAGE

Page 187

Jacqulynn Brookins
MY MENDED HEART

Page 192

> *Train up a child in the way he should go:
> and when he is old, he will not depart from it.*
> *-(Proverbs 22:6, KJV)*

THE BEGINNING ASKING JESUS IN
April Yarber

From the time I was young, I remember having a sense of *God around me*. I only went to a church a few times as a very young child with my grandmother Hazel.

My grandmother was always a strong believer in God. Although she did not share Him with the world, not my grandma. She worshipped and praised him in front of you, so you could see her dedication, but kept Him to herself. I believe I was about 4 or 5 years old when it happened, my first recollection of wanting to stand for God. I had gone with my grandma to church. I can still picture it. The little Baptist church that sat atop a hill which is located in a small town called, Rowland Heights, California. I remember I didn't want to sit in the main chapel pews with the big people (the grown-ups). I found it to be boring, so she sent me to Sunday school for the day. I still remember very clearly that time

I was there. The teacher had long pretty nails that she clacked on the back of the book that she was reading to the class. It was a bible story; it was the story of [2]*David and Goliath (HOLY BIBLE)*.

David was a little boy and was fighting against a giant. If you are not familiar with the story, I urge you to read it. I remember wanting to be [3]David. He was so brave and stood for God. He didn't seem to care that he was putting himself in danger and could possibly be killed by the giant. His focus wasn't on that, his focus was on God. David had such a fierce and awesome trust in God, he just knew that with HIM- *nothing* would be *impossible*. He didn't wait for the giant to approach, but instead, he faced his fear with courage and bravely charged forward. He didn't even put-on any earthly armor. But the giant was doomed, David had put on the only armor that mattered. He put on the armor of God. David trusted and was passionate about the confidence he had in the Lord, our God. He stepped out in faith in the most fearless way. I remember a feeling that came over me as she read, and for a

---

[2] 1 Samuel 17, DAVID AND GOLIATH

[3] 1 Samuel 17:50, NIV[50] *So David triumphed over the Philistine with a sling and a stone; without a sword in his hand he struck down the Philistine and killed him.*

moment I hoped someday I would get the chance to be brave and stand for God. I felt something as I hoped at that moment, but it quickly slipped away.

After the story she was standing next to me and looked over at me, she asked if I had asked Jesus into my heart? She explained to me what it meant to ask Him into your heart. She told me that Jesus loved me so much and that If I asked him into my heart, he would come and make a home in me, that he would always be with me.

So that day I did it, I asked *Jesus* into my *heart*.

I remember even then feeling a strong, joyful, emotion. I *wanted* His love and peace so bad. I think momentarily I remember even sensing His Presence. But that was such a quick glimpse, and I was so young. I didn't quite grasp the whole experience. I know I felt hopeful, I even cried happy tears. But I didn't notice or feel differently for long, not on that day, but later in my life, I would know. As now I have found hope in the days of the past, that at the time seemed so hopeless. At the time and in that moment, I couldn't see it before. But now I can see so clearly.

I can see that God *was* there, He was always there with me. Just as He *is* still with me today. He has been here *all along…*

Many times, in my life I have seen things and experienced things not of this world…Things with no explanation., things of what seemed at the time just coincidence. The *"what are the odds?"* type situations and experiences. Which I have felt, and always known in my deepest heart, it *is*, and *was*, and *will always be*, GOD.

Nothing to chance, not perhaps, not by accident, no nothing and no one could orchestrate life just the way the Father, our Savior, the Creator of all, has done and still does- today. I will share bits and pieces of what He has done for me and how His plan for me was all predesigned. Just like His plans for you. We all have a job, different jobs' but one purpose. His purpose given to us, to love and help spread the Gospel, which is the good news of Jesus Christ to everyone we meet. Hopefully planting good seeds which can lead them to Jesus and to His gift of Salvation…

What does it look like when we acknowledge and experience spiritual confirmation from God, well everyone is a little different.

Do you have any favorite number sequences?

I do- mine is 222

Before I begin here is something, I found interesting. It may mean something or nothing at all, but to me, it was just another way that God let me know that he knew and planned me to author this book and he chooses the order of the stories, not only for my book but in our lives. My favorite number for years has been 222. I have no idea why. No rhyme or reason just always have felt close to this number, and even wanted to be married on 2-22. So, if I would see it on a license plate or phone number, or just anywhere I would get that same feeling I get when I see hearts. I guess I'll call it that

"God is close feeling."

Well for Bill's story, I had a few additional questions, so we were emailing back and forth, and I noticed that in his email he had the number 222. So, it just so happened that on February-22 (which was coincidental I thought) I sent my uncle an email and I told him that 222 is my favorite number and asked him why it was in his email. He told me that it was his birthday. I never knew him, not even well enough to know his birthday, but here I was calling him on his birthday to ask about the number. Needless to say I got to wish him (for the very first time from me) a happy birthday. I really thought it was something. Here is how I see it...

HAPPY BIRTHDAY UNCLE BILL

the fact that I've always loved 222 and that it was Bill's birthday, and his was the first story that I chose for my book. It was a definite confirmation to me. This as well as every other thing in my life is all predesigned. This book I know I'm meant to write. So, when you are in doubt, let me reassure you, *Gods got a plan*. Just trust Him. But keep open those spiritual eyes, and in time He will reveal things to you that you may not have seen without those spiritual glasses on. And this we can read in the book of Daniel verse 2:22

He reveals deep and hidden things: he knows what lies in darkness, and light dwells in Him

-(Daniel 2:22, ESV)

Now we will start with Bill Sterling. This is my uncle who I never really got to see that much of while I was growing up, so I never really had the chance to get to know him. I felt so honored when my mother said that he had a story from his life to share for my book. It was so cool to sit down with him and really see him for the person he is, in just that short amount of time. Even though I do not know him more personally, we *are* family, and my soul does know his. We are family by more than blood, we are family because of Jesus Christ our Lord, and I know that this is all a part of God's plan, that this was all predesigned. I know in my heart that it is God's will that I get Bill's story, and Uncle Bill agrees.

> *They still bear fruit in old age; they are full of sap and ever green,*
> *-(Psalm 92:14, ESV)*

Me sitting down and talking to Uncle Bill…

Bill, who is now 82 years old recalls a time in his life where he felt the presence of something supernatural. But first, he shares a little with me about the present moments of his life. Bill sitting in his chair, back to the window. The sun beaming through.

He looks down at his hands... And begins, he starts by telling me about the daily frustrations that he has now, being his age. And with his memory problems setting in. He says," The worst thing I notice now is my memory... now I can remember what I did in high school, but yesterday is gone. It's aggravating. But then, I look around and I see people with, cancer, brain tumors, something that's going to kill them, and I think don't complain." Bill tells me that he just wants to make it to September. His wedding anniversary is in September, and he will have been married to Marlene for 62 years. I found this to be so touching- as this, you could tell was especially important to him. He stopped and paused for a second and added, " At this point in my life I'm not afraid to go.

Somedays I think I really have had enough, but then I think, there are so many people that would change places with me in a heartbeat. So, I say suck it up and move on. "Sometimes"... Bill pauses for a moment..."Sometimes, I'm hoping that I can, and everybody I know can, just go in their sleep. What more could you ask for?" Bill shared with me about his idea of dying," We all have a day, I believe. We just don't know when it is, but we all have a day and when it's your time, it's your time."

And the story begins…

THE SEMI-TRUCK INCIDENT
Bill Sterling

An Angel Perhaps…

Bill, who was living in West Virginia had been dating a nice girl named Marlene, and after she graduated high school in May they continued dating for the next few months. By September they got married, and they went on a four-day honeymoon from there they left for California. When they arrived in California, Bill had been offered a job driving a 40-foot semi-truck by a neighbor. Now before this, he had only experienced driving a small delivery truck.

This semi-truck carried these 70-foot-long steel beams. And on one trip he recalls that he had a full load. He had to travel from what he can recall through the grapevine in California. The grapevine some would say is the entire route of Interstate 5 from Castaic north to the San Joaquin Valley, but some say it is only a few steep miles from Fort Tejon to the bottom of the grade.

This is a steep 5 1/2-mile grade section at the northern end of this pass, so you can imagine what it would be like heading down the steep grade for this many miles in a huge truck with this kind of heavy load on it. For an inexperienced driver, pretty nerve-racking I'm assuming. And according to my uncle, it sounds as if I would be assuming correctly.

As Bill was heading down the grade, he could see the steel beams behind him. The ends of them all positioned facing towards the cab like huge steel stakes ready to impale him if anything went wrong.

As he descended the truck began to pick up speed. And he thought," Oh crap!" as by this time the truck was really going too fast to change any course of direction now, and if he braked too hard, he could lose total control and those beams could come unhitched and come crashing in, sliding through the rear window of the truck and take him out. But now he was going too fast so there was nothing he could do. He just had to concentrate on keeping the truck on the road. He was filled with fear.

As this was happening, he felt a strong *Presence* in the truck with him. He knew there was someone sitting in the passenger seat, but he was too scared to look over and see who it was." By this time, he was traveling at about 80 miles an hour or even faster as the speedometer only went to 80. He knew he had really made a stupid decision.

He thought about the Presence and said, "it could have been the devil saying, it was my day to die or an angel, but I was just too scared to look."

As he neared the mid to lower level of the incline, he knew he would have to swerve off and try to slow the truck using the side of the road. He heard his unknown passenger say, "It will be ok." Just then he did it, he swerved off. Most peculiar, but thankfully which seemed planned perfect timing there was a grate of gravel laid-out and an uphill slope. A place used to slow trucks, and this one was in just the *right* location at just this *perfect* time. This natural element of the gravel and the uphill climb began to slow the truck. Now his only focus was to regain control of the direction of the truck.

He would have just a bit of hope that he wouldn't crash if it responded to him. Which by the grace of God it had. As the truck finally slowed, he was able to stop. As he got out of the truck, a couple of passers-by came over to see if he was ok. When he stepped on the ground, he said his legs were shaky, but otherwise, he seemed to be ok.

Whether it was God himself or a guardian angel, Bill does not know. But what he does know is that his life was spared that day. And he told me it was the strangest thing that ever happened to him and said he wouldn't want to experience anything like that ever again.

Even to your old age and gray hairs
I am he, I am he who will sustain you.
I have made you and I will carry you;
I will sustain you and I will rescue you.
-(Isaiah 46:4, NIV)

✝

Another Story Comes
April Yarber

One of my dear friends, who is also my co-worker, Diane, had shared a very personal and touching story with me about the unimaginable true journey she went through with her son David, when he was just a small child.

At the time she had finally shared it with me in the office, several years had passed, but her emotional heartstrings, whenever she spoke of that time in her life, her words, and her memories still seemed so vivid. They would pull her back there to all those feelings that existed in those moments in time, and she would cry. Not only tears of sorrow as she remembered the pain and the fear of the situation, but she cried tears of joy and relief for everything she went through experienced and felt. She also cries tears even today, for the joy of being completely grateful to *Jesus Christ our Lord*, for the wonderful thing he has done for her and her son.

I had asked her if she wanted to share their story in this book when I started to write. I wasn't sure if she would. But today she handed me her story, in her words, and as I read it tears filled my eyes, I couldn't help but feel that much closer to her. My dear friend, my sister in Christ, Diane.

> [20] *"I do not ask for these only, but also for those who will believe in me through their word,* [21] *that they may all be one, just as you, Father, are in me, and I in you, that they also may be in us, so that the world may believe that you have sent me.* [22] *The glory that you have given me I have given to them, that they may be one even as we are one,* [23] *I in them and you in me, that they may become perfectly one, so that the world may know that you sent me and loved them even as you loved me.*
>
> *-(John 17:20-23, ESV)*

THE MIRACLE OF DAVID
Diane Reyes

My son David had always been a happy and healthy child. He had chubby rosy cheeks; he was just so cute.

One morning I was helping him get ready for preschool. I said to him "hurry up I need to change your clothes" I grabbed a nice shirt from his drawer, tried to put it on him but he wouldn't let me. He didn't want to wear the shirt I chose for him. We kept going back and forth about it. I said fine choose the one you want to wear. He got a green woody and buzz light year shirt. He looked so cute in it and off he went to school.

When my son was four years old, he was running around the house when suddenly I couldn't hear him anymore. I yelled, "Where's David?"…I heard the water running from down the hall. I walked towards the sound of the water which led me to the bathroom. Sure enough, I found him in there where he was playing with the water in the sink. It was filled with bubbly soap. "what are you doing?" I asked him. He turned around and looked at me.

To my surprise, his face was full of that soapy foam. I found it hilarious to see him with a huge bubbly beard he made himself. Then a few years later it happened…

The day it came…the dreaded day, it was the worst time in my life, it was the start of our *journey through the fire*…

One day I came home from work, I sat down next to my son on the couch while we watched a show on the television. I had my arm around my son's shoulder when he said to me, "Mom, I have something small on my neck." "What are you talking about, let me see" I demanded. When I looked at his neck I saw a tiny lump the size of a pea. I was dismissive, thinking it was nothing to worry about. Nevertheless, I told him, "I'll call the doctor to make an appointment."

A couple of days later I called and brought him in to get it checked out. After meeting with the doctor, he concluded it to be harmless but that he would still like to see him again for a follow-up. By the time my son and I met with his doctor for the second time, the lump was a little bigger.

This time around, the doctor prescribed my son antibiotics. Despite his effort, the lump continued to get bigger. Eventually, the antibiotics led to a rash. I brought him in again to see his doctor, but he insisted that we continue with the antibiotics. At this point, I grew terribly upset. I told him, "No! The antibiotics are giving him a rash." He was overtly upset with me for stopping the medication. But at this point, it did not matter to me what he thought because my motherly instincts said I need to get to the bottom of this. I needed to know what was happening to my son. Within the next days, several tests were taken, and the results showed everything was normal… until he was sent for a biopsy.

We drove to the doctor's office for the biopsy. I said, "Come on let's go we're going to be late." He got out of the car, saying, "Mom, I can't walk. "Confused and worried I told him, "What do you mean?" I rushed to his door and held him up. Most of his weight was on me, he was so weak. We slowly walked into the doctor's office. On top of this, he had a low-grade fever. The nurse in the biopsy room gave him Tylenol for it…

After I witnessed what had just happened, I knew something was not right. A few days later his primary doctor called me to make me an appointment to see the oncologist. Through all this mess, David had continued to go to school. One day he came home from school when I noticed he could barely carry his backpack. I said to him "What's wrong? Here sit down. "I offered him food and water, but he had no appetite. In fact, after I thought about it, I had noticed that he hadn't been really eating anything lately.

We walked into the Oncologists office to see what the results of the biopsy were. The Oncologist said, "We believe your son has some type of cancer, but we don't know what type. "We need to wait for more pathological results, but, you can go home, while we wait," he said… But I just couldn't wait any longer. David wasn't eating or drinking anything. So I told the Doctor that I would take him to the emergency room to see if someone else could tell me exactly what was going on." Finally the Doctor agreed and when he came back in the room he told me," We will be admitting your son to the hospital, we have a bed for him." By this time, the lump was the size of a softball. The doctors had to repeat the biopsy for a true final diagnosis, they were suspicious and knew that it was cancer.

The diagnosis came back on 4-25-2010. (*that date haunted me for the next several years.*)

The Doctor, and a social worker walked me into an empty room. We all sat down, I was just sad and scared, knowing that it was something bad.

He said the words, "Your son has *cancer.*"

I started shaking, my arms couldn't stop shaking. In a few days we would have a family meeting, with the doctors. My husband and I would be finding out the final diagnosis.

On the way to the meeting, I grabbed a towel from my son's room knowing that I would probably cry a lot. My husband and I anxiously walked into the meeting. Already there were some of my close family members and two Doctors plus the social worker. I couldn't find my sister, we were waiting for her to start, but she had been in the women's restroom crying. The doctors confirmed the cancer diagnosis…

My son David was diagnosed with Nasopharyngeal Carcinoma and Non-Hodgkin's Lymphoma stage 4, at the young age of 10 years old.

After the doctor spoke, each time I would cry over and over. He had to wait for me to stop crying, so that he could continue saying what he had to say next. It was the worst pain any human could endure. The world was spinning around in my head; it was overwhelming to hear. The pain was overbearing, and I was beyond myself with grief.

This was the absolute worst time in my life. I felt like I couldn't handle this news. It overwhelmed me so much that I felt dead-alive. I couldn't stop crying. I asked the Doctor," Do you think he will make it? Will he live?" …The Doctor said, "I don't know." The fact that he said he didn't know, gave me a little hope, but deep inside my heart and mind I was devastated…

The following weeks went by, we stayed in the hospital for more than 20 days straight the first time around. The Doctors' explained to David what was happening in a way he could understand. The Doctors' said, "You will need to cut your hair soon because your hair will start to fall out." He had a mohawk hairstyle at the time.

A volunteer hairstylist at the hospital cut David's hair short but not completely shaved like the doctor had asked.

He was so sad after his hair cut; he loved his hair so much. When we came back to the room, he was so upset that he covered his head with the bed sheets. Many days passed by, and no hair was falling out. Thank the Lord, his hair never fell out like the Doctors had said it would. He kept asking the doctors," When is my hair going to fall ,when will it fall, what day?"

The Doctors' were not sure why his hair or his eyelashes were not falling out, but they weren't, and thankfully they *never* did.

When his school friend Eric had come over to visit David. The only way David could communicate at that time was to write on a notepad. Due to his radiation, he had lost his voice for a whole week. He told his best friend Eric on the notebook "Do you want to play video games?" Or he would write to me, mom can you hand me the controller?

We lived in the hospital for a whole year.

A Porta-Cath and g-tube were placed in him. I remember when he got out of surgery after his port and g-tube were placed I waited in the lobby praying and praying, talking to God. The Doctor finally came out and said, "You can come in now surgery went well." When I walked to his bedside, I kissed his forehead and held his hand and when I peeked to look at his g-tube site the unimaginable pain and sadness hit me again like a stab in my heart. I felt no one could understand what I was dealing with because even though the family support was there, I couldn't stop feeling empty.

So later, I realized that *God* was the only one who truly understood what I was going through.

During that time, living there at the hospital, I had heard from some of the other moms that the same doctor that was treating David had given them a good prognosis for their children with stage 3 cancers. But even some of these children, I would witness die. It was heartbreaking.

My hope was fading, but deep within my heart I knew what I had to do, and who I had to go to for help. It was the Lord; He is who I needed to seek and ask for help. The Lord was the only Doctor that would give me hope. And so, I went to Him, to save my sons life. I humbly asked God," Please heal my son David and save him in the name of Jesus Christ." I prayed tirelessly, I trusted God with my whole heart, mind, and soul, I asked God for His mercy.

At the hospital I would sleep next to my son in a recliner chair. The chair was next to a window. One early morning at 6 am, I awoke, I opened my eyes, and the curtains were pulled open, so I was able to look out through the window. When I looked out, I saw a beautiful big palm tree right in front of David's room. What I saw next that morning, while looking out the window at the palm tree was the most miraculous thing you could ever imagine seeing.

I saw an image of *Jesus's face* manifest in the tree.

The palm tree branches clearly formed His face. The shape of His eyebrows, His eyes, nose, mouth, and His hair. I recognized that face, it was the face of our Savoir in the tree. He was even wearing the crown of thorns on his forehead. I stared at the image and couldn't believe my eyes! I thought to myself… if I just close my eyes for a second it might be gone, but if it is still here when I open them again, it will just have to be real…Not believing it would still be there, I did it. I closed my eyes and when I opened them again, it was still there.

Jesus's face stood before me like a light of hope.

I know now that this was my sign that my son David *would* live. I stared at it for as long as I could, imprinting it in my memory. Slowly the image began to fade away, but it left me with such peace.

Seeing Jesus gave me more than hope, He gave me *peace*.

It was then that I knew that Jesus would save my son. It was a miracle only meant for my eyes to see. I knew when I told people they might not believe me, so I only shared my experience with my close family. I found comfort knowing that my family would believe me and that this could provide them with hope and comfort as well.

From that day forward I knew in my heart that my son would get well. Sometimes people may see a cloud in the shape of a heart or something they hold dear; this was remarkably similar to that but so vivid and alive. I'm not sure if while you're reading this you will fully understand or believe me, but I wanted to share this truth, sharing the hope that the Lord provided for me during a time I needed Him most. A hope that is available to us all, we just need to believe and be open to receive Him. We all see God winks and experience miracles every day we just need to open our spiritual eyes and pay close attention. God is always with us, and sometimes He will pull back His perfect veil to reveal Himself to us.

Months later when we were told that David was cancer- free. David told me a part of his story that at the time I did not know, but now it makes sense. He said," Mom, do you remember when my hair didn't fall out?' I said," Yeah, but why are you bringing that up now?" David whispered to me," *I prayed to God to please don't let my hair fall out, not my hair.*" I was like wow… "You are funny, but indeed God did listen to you."

> *And his name—by faith in his name—has made this man strong whom you see and know, and the faith that is through Jesus has given the man this perfect health in the presence of you all.*
>
> *-(Acts 3:16, ESV)*

He saved my son David's life and now he has been cancer- free for over 10 years…

After all David's cancer treatments, high doses of radiation, and the chemo treatments were done, the Doctors said that most likely my son David would never be able to have any children. We were given the option of doing a fertility test. But we decided not to. We decided that we would worry about that later in life.

I knew of another child who went through something similar to David, he had done the test and found out that he would *never* have children. I prayed again many prayers asking God to let David be able to have children. Although it wasn't planned and my son is still very young, David has fathered a child. A little girl, who looks a lot like him….

Now I have a *miracle son* and a *miracle granddaughter*.

And an added dedication to my beautiful miracle granddaughter Evangeline,
You are so very loved, love Grandma Diane

Scripture Share

MY REFUGE AND MY FORTRESS-

He who dwells in the shelter of the most High will abide in the shadow of the Almighty. I will say to the Lord, "My refuge and my fortress, my God, in whom I trust." For He will deliver you from the snare of the fowler and from the deadly pestilence. He will cover you with His pinions, and under His wings you will find refuge; His faithfulness is a shield and buckler.

You will not fear the terror of the night, nor the arrow that flies by day, nor the pestilence that stalks in darkness, nor the destruction that wastes at noonday. A thousand may fall at your side, ten thousand at your right hand, but it will not come near you. You will only look with your eyes and see the recompense of the wicked. Because you have made the Lord your dwelling place-the Most High, who is my refuge-no evil shall be allowed to befall you, no plague come near your tent. For he will command his angels concerning you to guard you in all your ways. On their hands they will bear you up, lest you strike your foot against a stone...

You will tread on the lion and the cobra; the young lion and the serpent you will trample under foot."

Because he holds fast to me in love, I will deliver him; I will protect him, because he knows my name. When he calls to me, I will answer him; I will be with him in trouble; I will rescue him and honor him. With long life I will satisfy him and show him my salvation."

- (Psalm 91, ESV)

Encouragement

My message to you is to *seek* God, for whatever you need, in whatever you're facing. Jesus Christ is a healer, He is forgiving. He is loving, kind, merciful and miraculous. God is good all the time. I am forever thankful and grateful to God, that through the gift of His Son Jesus, he saved mine.

Gratefully-Diane

The Lord brought me another story
April Yarber

How I met Shirl…

Another weekend was coming and this weekend my fiancé James and I were invited to go to his sister's birthday barbeque. He doesn't get to see his sister a lot or his two beautiful nieces because they live out of state. They were here for a short visit to celebrate with the family, so he was looking forward to seeing the girls.

During the week, my babe had noticed a rash on his inner thigh It was making him feel a little anxious. On Friday night we googled rashes and as many of you know, the worst of the worst showed up on the many possibilities of what it could be. It left James overwhelmed with anxiety.

So, Saturday was here, and we got ready to go to the party. After he got ready, he looked at me and said he didn't want to go. He was having anxiety and wanted to see what the rash was. He called his sister and informed her that we wouldn't be coming but instead, we were going to go to the Doctor's. There was an urgent care that was open just down the street. We went to the urgent care and when the Doctor came in and saw it, she intuitively knew what it was. He had shingles. It wasn't anything to worry about it and was only contagious if someone touched it directly. She gave him medication that would help him get well faster. We decided it was probably a blessing not to be going to the party since there were a lot of little children and babies there. Plus, all the kids, especially his nieces, like to climb all over him. So, it probably wouldn't have been the best idea to go.

Since we were all ready to go out, and I was a bit hungry, I suggested we go out to eat. Usually, I am more of a homebody so getting me to go anywhere, even to dinner is exceedingly rare. But on this day, I asked him if we could go to a restaurant that I had been to with my bible study ladies a few months earlier. It was a little Mexican restaurant near our home. I can't tell you what made me choose this place, it wasn't a place that I ever decided to go to on my own, but this day it seemed like a good idea to me. So, we decided we would go and if it wasn't crowded, we would eat there. Mind you this was a Saturday night, so I had it in my mind that it was probably going to be crowded and that we would not be eating there. But when we got there, low and behold, it wasn't crowded. We walked in and got seated right away. We were seated in a cute little booth and across from us a little to my left sat a sweet lady and her son. They were enjoying their dinner and engaging in a deep conversation.

After we ordered, James and I were talking and suddenly I heard the lady from across the way say something that got my attention. She had said something about the Holy Spirit and how you know when he's leading you or something to that effect. Instantly a feeling came over me I knew why we were there. I told my Fiancé that I felt like I needed to talk to her. I said," My Holy Spirit is tugging at my heart, I need to go over there." James looked at me and said, " babe leave them alone." We chuckled as I responded, "You want me to ignore my Holy Spirit? 'Just then I heard the lady mention a time when she felt she had died and experienced a near- death experience. I looked at James and said," That's it, that's confirmation*! She's the reason we're here*. I'm supposed to get her story for my book. I have to go over there." James agreed as he knew that I was being led by the Holy Spirit.

I bravely got up and walked over to the table. The lady and her son were still involved in what seemed to be a quite deep conversation, so I felt a little intrusive, but I knew that it was important.

As I got up to the table, I waited for a second for them to notice me. I said, " Excuse me, my- name is April, and I know- this may sound a little odd, but I'm writing a Christian anthology book series called 'Speaking to the Heart from Flicker to Flame.' I explained what the book series was about and added, I know this may sound unbelievable but I was drawn to you. I felt led to come talk to you by my Holy Spirit. "This I thought could have gone one of two ways but I didn't let fear stop me as I knew who it was that had sent me to her and thankfully it didn't seem to put her off.

She introduced herself to me as Shirl, "the Book Doctor." In my hearts- mind, I felt like my actions were confirmed once again. As she told me she was a *Christian* book editor, and I was thinking that it was such perfect timing and that I would probably need her services for this book in the future. I explained how I had overheard her speak of the Holy Spirit and how I felt led to her. What I didn't explain was exactly what I had experienced. When she was talking about the Holy Spirit, I heard the word,' Listen' followed by a pull in my spirit, almost like an inner voice that nudged me as it said- 'pay attention.'…

I knew in my heart that I needed to talk to her, but then I felt a pause of fear momentarily, and again while I was contemplating going over, I had overheard her say something about her near-death experience and that's when it was *clear*.

It *was* confirmation to me without a doubt, that I needed to get her story for my book. But only if she would be willing to share? I told her to pray about it. She accepted my offer right there and then. She went on to tell me she had a *couple* of stories to contribute to the series. I was astonished and grateful to the Lord for His provision. When she gave me her business card it hit home even more .

'The Book Doctor' is what it says. Shirl Thomas the book editor.

When the Lord leads listen without worry or hesitation and amazing things happen as He reveals His plan…

> *And my God will supply every need of yours according to his riches in glory in Christ Jesus.*
> *-(Philippians 4:19, ESV)*

When she and her son were ready to leave, they passed by our table to say goodbye. She stood up next to me. We exchanged pleasantries and then she paused, put her hand on my shoulder looked me in the eyes smiled, and said, "*Walk with Jesus.*" Of course, I thought I knew what she meant, but really didn't until I read her stories. She sent her stories to me shortly thereafter by email, since she is an editor, I won't change a thing, I will copy and paste her contributions into the book.

In Loving Memory of Shirl Thomas

Before this book was published Shirl Thomas passed away, and although I didn't get to know her in this life I believe she is with our Lord in heaven just *walking with Jesus* . I read a segment from an article about her showing the kind of person she was Her favorite saying tells it all…

"I complained I had no shoes, until I met a man with *no feet.*"

Shirl was a mother, grandmother, and great-grandmother, known as "Mom, Mama, Mama-San, Oma, Ga, and Grammy."

May your family be comforted Shirl, and another angel receives her wings,..

> [3] He heals the brokenhearted
> and binds up their wounds.
> -(Psalm 147:3,ESV)

> [4] "Blessed are those who mourn,
> for they shall be comforted.
> -(Matthew 5:4, ESV)

Let us take a moment to say a prayer for her family and surround them with Gods love. And as we read her contributions you can see that she was given a glimpse of what lies just on the other side of the veil. Only the Lord and His great provision, being outside of time, could provide something that most of us would call...

Truly MIRACULOUS...

A LIGHT OF PEACE
Shirl Thomas

A few years ago, while riding my exercise bike, a strange feeling came over me. And, suddenly, I guess I blacked out because I felt like I'd moved to a completely peaceful place and saw a bright light – kind of like through a tunnel. Then, just as suddenly, I was aware of being back on my bike, and felt disappointed, because I preferred to be back where it was so peaceful. It was probably only a few seconds, but it felt glorious.

> ^{78} *because of the tender mercy of our God,*
>   *by which the rising sun will come to us from heaven*
> ^{79} *to shine on those living in darkness*
>   *and in the shadow of death,*
> *to guide our feet into the path of peace."*
>
> *-(Luke 1:78-79, NIV)*

JESUS MY COMPANION
Shirl Thomas

Many years ago, I went to a Christian Writers' Conference and mingled with many writers, all of different faiths, and creating prose for God. At the time, I was much younger, and walked every morning. Being in Arizona at a gathering made no difference. I awakened early and took my walk. A young man came walking toward me, obviously taking his morning walk also.

He smiled, raised his hand, and said, *"Walk with Jesus"*. . .

At that moment in the dry Arizona dirt, a footprint appeared directly in the front of my feet, and I got chills knowing it was our Lord walking with me.

Shirl Thomas

It is absolutely amazing how God works out all the little details of the day, to get us to that right place, at just the right moment…

It's truly fascinating to think about. Our Lord is just that way. He gets it done; He is truly creative in the ways in which He accomplishes things. Makes sense, as now I am chuckling at myself, (like hello April) He is the *Creator*.

Another Divine Appointment
April Yarber Berg

How I met Mason…

I was at work, but something that day with my breathing wasn't feeling right. I couldn't seem to catch my breath, no matter how deep a breath I would take. I felt like I wasn't getting the oxygen I needed. I felt lightheaded and was afraid I'd pass out.

My co- workers who are like a second family to me were worried about me too. They told me to go to the emergency room. Usually, I am not one to go to the ER. I would usually go to the urgent care through my primary care doctor's office or do nothing at all and simply just tough it out, but this day I was so afraid. One of my co-workers Fabi asked me if she could take me to the ER, and this time I agreed.

I was scared that I might just pass out if I walked by myself.

It was so kind that she offered to take me. So, I reluctantly agreed to go with her. I clocked out for the day, and she walked me over to the ER. I felt like I couldn't answer the questions of the admitting staff, so Fabi did it for me while I sat and waited in the waiting room. After I was all checked in, Fabi went back to work, every so often the ER staff would come to get me and do tests that were ordered. In between the tests, I would find myself back in the waiting room. Feeling a little better, I struck up a conversation with a guy who was very nice. His name was Mason. On the 2nd or 3rd time I was placed back in the waiting-room, Mason was still there. I believe or conversation turned to God. So he started to share a true story about a time in his life with me. It was about a time he had experienced without knowing it, an angel.

That's when it dawned on me and I *knew* in my heart as I felt again that familiar internal tug, I was here to get his story for my book.

I explained to him that I was authoring this book and asked if he wouldn't mind sharing his story in it. He said he would be honored.

So, we exchanged phone numbers and I told him I would contact him later for the story…

I had just one more test to do, when my fiancé James had shown up in the waiting room, I introduced him to Mason, and they talked while I went back for my last test. After that I was feeling much better and yes, just as you could have guessed, all the tests were normal, and I was released to go home.

On the way home I thought about the way the Lord had gotten me to the ER so that I could meet Mason and get his story. I looked up, smiled, and said, "Thank you Lord for giving me such a beautiful, good purpose. Also thank you that *nothing* is wrong with me, I am ok. Did I really have to go to the ER? I chuckled to myself and thought …

Jesus, I love you.

> [5] *Trust in the* LORD *with all your heart,*
> *and do not lean on your own understanding.*
> [6] *In all your ways acknowledge him,*
> *and he will make straight your paths.*
> -(Proverbs 3:5-6, ESV)

✝

IN THE ARMS OF AN ANGEL
Mason Zepeda

The year was 1989 and I was living in Newport Beach while attending Orange Coast College. It was between the evening hours of 8 and 9 pm, I had just bought a new motorcycle. I drove up to a four- way stop sign intersection in Newport Beach, around the area where I was living. My friend Kevin was on the back of my motorcycle as my passenger.

Suddenly, I was *struck* from behind by a red truck!

My friend Kevin and my motorcycle went forward veering to the left and crashed on the street. The red truck went forward veering out to the right eventually skidding to a stop. I saw the whole accident from high up above. Instantly, I was back on the ground on my feet. I must have been in shock! I do not know how I was up above and didn't feel anything holding onto me. I should have flown the way my motorcycle and my friend Kevin had, but I didn't…

I watched the whole accident take place from high up above seemingly from a safe distance. When I was back on my feet I started walking over to see if my friend Kevin and the driver of the red truck were ok. A girl ran over to me and was grabbing my shoulder and arm.

The girl kept saying over and over, "Oh my God, the ANGEL was so big that lifted you, did you see it? The Angel was so big!"

Just then the red truck takes off! Two of my college friends that were on the corner at the time of the accident, jumped in the back of the red truck as it left. They were pounding on the back window of the cab with their hands yelling for him to stop. The driver of the red truck got pulled over and was arrested for drunk driving, hit, and run and endangering the lives of others while speeding. Amazingly, neither Kevin nor I had a scratch on our bodies.

For he will command His angels concerning you to guard you in all your ways.

-(Psalm 91:11, ESV)

Ever since I could remember I've always felt a strong connection and relationship with God. After the angel incident, I had belief without a doubt in my heart and soul of God's Divine and Holy intervention.

Always, Mason

The Butterfly People
April Yarber

Divine appointments are beautiful just like butterflies, they appear almost out of nowhere...

When I met Priscilla and Joe" the Butterfly People,"

I met a beautiful couple a few years ago. From the moment I met them I felt a closeness, almost family-like... Just sitting there, he reminded me so much of my Poor papaw (my grandpa Clarence.) Maybe it was because he was so skinny with big brown eyes, just like my grandpa. There was something so familiar about these two, and I felt a sense of peace around this couple. I do not remember how we started to speak of God, but of course, we did. We spoke of how amazing God is and of how HE is so important in our lives. Then they told me that they do something else that is amazing and beautiful. They have an organization to save the Monarch butterflies. That is where I came up with their nicknames.

They are the "*butterfly people.*" Priscilla, the butterfly lady, and Joe, the butterfly man. And their hearts and spirits are beautiful, just like the monarch butterflies.

Sadly, not too long after I met them Joe had passed away, but my babe and I did get to go to one of their events in Newport Beach, where they let us feed watermelon to the butterflies in a tent with little plastic forks. The butterflies would land on the watermelon, and you could walk around the tent with them carefully until they would fly off and land elsewhere.

Joe and Priscilla educated us on what we could do to help the monarchs. I admired them and their purpose. Joe even spoke in front of the crowd about how special the Monarchs are, and he let all these little kids set the monarch butterflies free in the sky to fly along the coast and migrate. It was amazing to watch. Pricilla and I have stayed friends, she is my sister in Christ. I shared with her about this book I am working on, and she said she would love to contribute one of her stories.

I must admit, now every time that I see a monarch butterfly, I think of Joe and of how his spirit is free to fly. I think of how beautiful his love for Pricilla was. I often wonder if God lets our loved ones watch over us, using the birds and butterflies, as if to say," Hello, I love you, you're not alone. Don't worry there's more, and the best is yet to come." Anyhow, I know there is no sadness on their side of the fence, but it is so comforting for us to think about, isn't it? And in those moments that something like this happens, you see a hummingbird, or a butterfly, or just something in nature and think of a relative or loved one that has passed on. Your soul ties them together. It brings comfort, doesn't it? And at that moment, you feel their peace, which brings you a sense of comfort, and I believe that is why it happens…

God allows it. He allows it for us because He loves us. And no-good thing does God withhold from us.

> *For the LORD God is a sun and shield; the Lord bestows favor and honor. No good thing does He withhold from those who walk upright.*
>
> *-(Psalm 84:11, ESV)*

This day Priscilla emailed me her story, and these are her words...

THE VISION
Priscilla James- Cruz

"This is what the Lord help me to write and even told me when. *God is Great All the Time!!*"

I HAVE A BADGE WITH THE WORDS "Don't Keep the Faith -Spread it."

I do not know where I got the badge, or how or when. I do know why I got it. I have this badge out in[4] sight in my kitchen where anybody that enters my kitchen can see it. I see it constantly whenever I am in my kitchen, my eyes glance in that direction. That is what I just did a few minutes ago which is why I am writing this today. I want to spread my faith to others for them to feel the love of our God, Jesus, and the Holy Spirit/Ghost

---

[4] MATTHEW 13:16-17,*ESV*[16] *But blessed are your eyes, for they see, and your ears, for they hear.* [17] *For truly, I say to you, many prophets and righteous people longed to see what you see, and did not see it, and to hear what you hear, and did not hear it.*

in case they have not recognized receiving His loving touch when it was sent to them in their daily walk of life…

I will share one of my latest times when I was asked to be strong in my faith…

It was a month ago and I was staying at my son's and daughter-in law's home because of the respiratory disease, the COVID-19, also known as the Coronavirus. A few days after I went there my son was told he had been in contact with someone that had been tested for the virus and the test had come back positive. Immediately my son went and got tested for the virus and was told he would find out the results in two days.

Now the plan set forth for the next two days was for my daughter-in-law and myself to be separated from my son, which we set about to do. I gave him my bedroom, which they had made for me, which had a closed door, and I took the couch, in the living room, to sleep on while we waited the two days. During the wee early hours of the second day, I am lying awake, as I usually do because that seems to be my spiritual quiet time. It's a time that I can hear the best, and I started going over the present situation in my mind.

I started thinking about my daughter-in-law and how we had time these past two days to share our faith. We both had been praying for the results of the test to be negative. And it was so sad, so very sad to not be able to hug or see my son. I didn't even talk to him for the last two days. I could only hear him open the door to pick up and to receive the plates of food that his wife had cooked and left for him, and then close the door again. I started questioning in my mind laying there, would it even be two days or longer?

I knew I had to turn it over to *God* at this point because He was in control.

Again I found myself praying and talking to our Lord. I asked if it would be His will, that this separation could end quickly, and whenever we would be notified I asked that He help us accept the outcome. Then my thoughts went to how my son might be notified by phone or email and thinking he would come out of the room and tell us, at that point is when I would know.

Then I had a spiritual vision of him coming out of the room going to his wife who had her back to him, he walked over to her, as he reached her putting his arms around her waist and hugging her and I would be in view to see it happen, just keep the faith

(as I am writing this my eyes are tearing and can hardly see the words I am putting down on paper because that is *exactly* what happened.)

As the day, March 22, 2020, the second day of waiting went on, sometime in- the afternoon, I am sitting at the kitchen table, my daughter-in-law is doing something at the sink with her back to the bedroom door (here I go again, tearing) I didn't hear the door open, but I see my son walk over toward the sink and I'm thinking he can't be in the kitchen, by then I see him reach for my daughter-in-law's waist, hugs her, and turns her around, she asks him "you ok?" and receives his long-awaited hug…

I see this happening and now I know all is ok and I run over, with great excitement, to join in the hugs, and we are all hugging, crying, and thanking God!!

And yes, faith did get us through those two days. Just passing it on to all those who believe and to those who do not believe and to those who might be on the fence of believing. I might add, I was not supposed to be at my son's house. My daughter picked me up to stay at their house to keep me safe from being in contact with anybody that might have the virus, but she found out when she returned to her work that someone there had been in contact with someone that had the virus, and she wanted my son-in-law to take me to my son's house before she got home…

Now my daughter-in-law has gone back to her job. I am back in my own home, going about life in my own kitchen, and my eyes again catch sight of this badge with the words,

"DON'T KEEP the FAITH -SPREAD it."
I BELIEVE THAT IS HOW THE HOLY SPIRIT WORKS IN MY LIFE!!

Love and Blessings Priscella

In Loving memory of Joe "The Butterfly Man."

And the dust returns to the earth as it was, and the spirit returns to God who gave it.
           - (Ecclesiates 12:7, ESV)

HE CALLS ME OUT OF THE MUCK
April S. Yarber

JESUS speaks to my heart…

Oh my precious little child, so lost and in so much pain. Shh… listen, open your heart to hear. My plans are not to hurt you or to watch you suffer, but instead, they are for your building up, pruning, and refining, as you are *not alone* in the fire. I have great plans for you. Oh, why do you let go of my hand and bury your faith under all that is hopeless? I will restore you, if only you will listen, repent, and come follow me.

> *And after you have suffered a little while, the God of all grace, who has called you to his eternal glory in Christ, will himself restore, confirm, strengthen, and establish you.*
> *-(1 Peter 5:10, ESV)*

There was a significantly horrible time in my life, at the time I was a young woman. I drank and did drugs and had been caught in the snare of the enemy. I was naive. And fell into the trap of drinking first, then eventually doing drugs. I was enchanted and deceived by the illusion that this way of life was normal and fun. I ended up like so many who start off innocently enjoying the party. It drained me of my spirit, and it robbed me. It robbed me of ME, and ruined for a time, many of my relationships. I was so *lost*.

Although I always felt Jesus trying to get my attention, I pushed Him away, trying to separate Him from my life. Trying to hide the person I was, and what I was doing from Him and my loved ones.

My life had never been easy and there are so many things that I cannot bear to talk about, not even to this day, things that are too hard, things that I'm not ready to share, as it is too painful to relive. But during these times, I wasn't even recognizable to myself.

I was so angry at God. But He *didn't give up* on me.

Even though I had denounced Him, during one of my drug-induced self-pitiful, crying fits. He never stopped loving me. He forgave me, just as He forgave Peter in the bible.

For those of you that aren't that familiar yet with Peter. He was one of the Lord's [5]Apostles. One of His closest and dearest followers,` more than that, Peter and Jesus were best friends. But giving into the fear in a situation,[6] Peter had denied even knowing Jesus, not once or twice but three times. And then Peter cried (I'm sure he felt guilt, sadness, and shame)…But what do you think Jesus did? What was his reaction, do you think Jesus forgave Peter? Well yes, he forgave him, Jesus restored Peter. This is just the way the Lord is. He never gives up on his children. He forgives us and gives to us His mercy and grace. Waiting for us to admit our wrongs, turn away from our sin and seek Him.

---

[5] Merrium -Webster definition **Apostle** - **a:** one sent on a mission: such as **b:** one of an authoritative New Testament group sent out to preach the gospel and made up especially of Christ's 12 original disciples and Paul

[6] LUKE 22:61-62 [61] *And the Lord turned and looked at Peter. And Peter remembered the saying of the Lord, how he had said to him, "Before the rooster crows today, you will deny me three times."* [62] *And he went out and wept bitterly.*

If He had let me go back then, I would have been lost forever. But He didn't and I'm grateful. He revealed Himself several times, trying to save me, trying to open my eyes. And here was one of those times, that in the moment that it was happening I momentarily felt the power, but couldn't truly understand the significance. Although in hindsight, as people rightfully say 20/20 is perfect vision.

This time looking back at a bigger view of the picture, well, I can see that it is/was…a clear vision of God's Provision, and the anointing of His perfect love…

> *And I will lead the blind in a way that they do not know, in paths that they have not known I will guide them. I will turn the darkness before them into light, the rough places into level ground. These are the things I do, and I do not forsake them.*
> *-(Isaiah 42:16, ESV)*

ANNOINTED WITH LOVE
April Yarber

This is very hard for me to write and share, because of my shame, but I feel it is necessary… so here it goes.

One morning early I had been up all-night partying, drinking and doing drugs (yikes that feels so horrible to say/write or even think about, but it is the truth and so necessary.)

I was in a neighborhood about twenty- minutes away from my aunts. At this time, I was homeless. It was a little before five in the morning, as I walked through a neighborhood in Ontario, California. As I walked, I noticed spray painting and graffiti all over the brick walls which were on both sides of the street, and I briefly thought' this probably wasn't the best area to be walking around on foot in.'

A lot of the writing was evil. I saw 666 and demon night and the words, evil lives. Ugly spray-painted demon faces and horrible images. I felt a huge amount of anxiety inside, in this moment I was filled with the fear of evil. I was always scared of the devil. I prayed aloud in my mind asking God to make sure that no one who could harm me was out here.

As I walked, my heart was nervously beating harder, and I began walking even faster and picked up my speed. It was like walking in a nightmare, like some kind of horror movie. The sky above was still kind of dark and the air was brisk. Even though I was walking fast, I felt like I was walking in slow motion. An array of thoughts filled my head. Thoughts about the wrong I was doing and where my life was headed? It was really early morning, so the sun hadn't fully come out. I was walking in the quiet before the rest of the world woke up. Just then I heard a voice from across the street. Thankfully, it was a lady's voice calling out to me.

"Young girl there, hey young girl, where are you going?... You know God's got plans for you, you just have to get your priorities straight. Come over here."

I don't know why I went to her. Maybe because she seemed older, which made her more trustworthy, she was like "Mother-Ish" and in all honesty, I was scared. There was just something about her that felt peaceful and safe. I walked up to her, and she started to tell me that Jesus loved me. She asked me why I was out and living this way? I had no answers for her. She pointed out a necklace I was wearing and told me- it was deceiving and represented evil, she said that I should throw it away. It was a silver necklace and on it a jester, a king's clown, from the medieval days. She said even something as little as this could be influencing me with its negative symbolism. Its symbol was that of a fool, I took it off and handed it to her. We walked over to a dumpster and she took it and threw it away that moment.

> *You will also defile the covering*
> *of your images of silver,*
> *And the ornament of your molded*
> *images of gold.*
> *You will throw them away as an*
> *unclean thing;*
> *You will say to them, "Get away!"*
> *-(Isaiah 30:22, NKJV)*

Then we turned and I followed her to her apartment. As she went in, I waited outside near the door. She walked into her house and grabbed a bottle of oil. I had never heard of anointing before, and at the time did not really understand the significance of this either. She began praying over me and anointed my head with oil. With her finger she put a cross on my head with the oil. I felt very strange and overwhelmed with emotion. My tears began to flow, and I began to cry, for several moments I couldn't stop the tears. Even though I felt the weight of all my shame, I also felt a small sense of hope restored. Maybe things would be alright, but I was still lost inside, and it would be a long while before I straightened out my life. It would be a long crazy journey before I got my *"priorities straight."*

> *But the anointing that you received from him abides in you, and you have no need that anyone should teach you. But as his anointing teaches you about everything, and is true, and is no lie—just as it has taught you, abide in him.*
> *-(1 John 2:27, ESV)*

Today I wish I knew the lady's name, and I wonder if she still lives there. I would like to thank her because I know that her words in that moment significantly changed something for me.

That anointing I received was something that I now cherish. What was it like in that moment ? Well, if I could explain it…

It was as if I felt *God draw me near to HIM*. It was a closeness to God that I can't fully explain.

Just in that moment, although I was a mess, I had a glimpse of *peace,* and I knew deep inside that someday it would all be alright. Speaking with the lady well, it was like truly talking to an angel. Which I have wondered maybe she was. All I know is that I will never forget her, or that morning, for all of my life. The morning that I was shown grace and was anointed with God's love.

They say God always takes you back in ministry to the places you came from. I know this to be true I have a heart for addicts and for people who feel lost, out of control, and unlovable, being there myself and walking in the dark for quite some time. If you are struggling or know someone who struggles… please read or have them read the letter on the next few pages of truth… a message sent with love from my heart to you, whomever you are…

Always In His service, April~

✝

A LETTER OF ENCOURAGEMENT TO THOSE WHO SUFFER FROM ADDICTION

To Anyone feeling helpless, (*God* is your *Help*, Seek Him)

To Those who are feeling powerless, (Almighty *God* is All-*Powerful*, Draw near to Him)

To Someone feeling hopeless, (*Jesus* is *Hope*, hold onto Him)

To my Brothers and Sisters, who are having a hard time coping with life, who may be struggling with addiction or any other stronghold. I want you to know, *you can and shall overcome this* with JESUS.

Keep your eyes up and find hope in the Lord. He is your confidence! Wrap yourself in His words, which are found within the pages of The Bible, let Him soak you in His perfect love.

[7]JESUS loves you! [8]

He has forgiven you.

---

[7]Jeremiah 31:3, ESV- *The LORD appeared to him from far away. I have loved you with an everlasting love; therefore I have continued my faithfulness to you.*

[8] 1 John 1:9, ESV- *If we confess our sins, He is faithful and just to forgive us our sins and to cleanse us from all unrighteousness.*

All of it is *forgiven*.

Just surrender and Ask Him into your heart, as your Lord. He is your Salvation, and He is your Savior. Ask Him for His strength and to protect you from all temptations.

Rebuke the enemy and all the unclean spirits trying to control you using the power of the Holy Spirit.

Right now, you may be weak, but He is strong, and He shall help you see your breakthrough. He will break all generational curses. Also the strongholds of addictions and the bad habits will fall off of your life. Only… will you let him? Hold Him tightly soak in His words. He is with you and for you ! No weapon formed against you shall prosper. But don't give up !!!!

For just as surely as the sun will rise tomorrow, no matter how horrible your life may be this day- Hold on I say! For there will come a day… if you do *not* give up when you shall see the beauty in this life that GOD has created and designed just for YOU.

You will see it through sober eyes, and you *will* work hard to obtain all that GOD has placed in your HEART and called you to do/be

… and you *will* be FREE. No longer will you be a muted version of yourself, but you will be the true, beautiful, you, that God created. You will shine with the vibrant colors of joy and love that the enemy stole away some time ago. You will get them back and shine even brighter than before.

> So if the Son sets you free, you will be free indeed.
> -(John 8:36, NIV)

You will be free, and you will experience the love of God- maybe for the first time in your life, you will know what it feels like to truly be loved, and you will understand that *you* are an amazing creation with a beautifully designed purpose…

GOD, the creator of heaven and earth- CHOSE to create one of YOU…

You are truly that special to HIM

As always with love, April

P.S. Keep those Eyes up, Hearts open, and Confidence in the LORD!

> *And after you have suffered a little while, the God of all grace, who has called you to His eternal glory in Christ, will himself restore, confirm, strengthen, and establish you.*
>
> *-(1 Peter 5:10, ESV)*

If you do not know Jesus as your Lord and Savior, and are ready to turn your life over to Him, just pray the prayer on the next page and you will be born again…[9]

---

[9] John 3:3 *Jesus replied, "Very truly I tell you, no one can see the kingdom of God unless they are born again." (NIV)*

Dear Heavenly Father,

I believe that Jesus died for me. I believe that Jesus paid for my sins on the cross. I believe that Jesus rose from the dead. I ask you to forgive me of my sins. I ask you to wash me clean of all sin.

I put my faith and trust in Jesus as my only hope for living eternally with you in heaven.

I ask Jesus to be my Savior and my Lord. I want to live my life for Christ.

I understand that my salvation is not based on my works but on the sacrifice of Jesus on the cross.

Thank you for saving me!

Amen![10]

---

[10] This prayer was copied from the internet. I neglected to save the author's name along with the prayer but would like to thank him as I have used this prayer many times when leading people to Christ.

My Beautiful Aunt and Uncle
April Yarber

My Aunt Colleen has shared with me that she has a story to share for this book about a time in her life where the Lord showed up in the most peculiar way. It is a story about the comfort that He can bring. My aunt, when I was younger was always watching out for me during my early teenage years. She and my uncle Clay lived across the street from me and my dad, who was a hard worker, and was gone a lot... So they would supervise me when they could. My Uncle Clay would always talk to me about the Lord, and my aunt Colleen would hunt me down from places that I shouldn't have been, such as parties. They have helped me in my life. Colleen and Clay have so many amazing stories of God's love to share, and here is one of her stories about how something so small can have such a big impact....

> *Beside them the birds of the heavens dwell;*
> *they sing among the branches.*
> *- (Psalm 104:12, ESV)*

BLUE-BIRD ON MY SHOULDER
Colleen Rosencrans

I woke up one morning and I was not able to get out of bed. This was something that I have *never* experienced before. I felt like I was having a *heart attack*. I was so weak. I was worried so I laid there in bed for a long while.

Then something caught my attention, it was the sound of knocking on the window of my room. The noise took my attention away from what I was feeling. I got myself up and out of bed to see what it was. As I got near to my window…there he was, a bluebird looking in at me and chirping as if he had something to say.

As I stared at him, I began to feel better. I got up and went into the living room and sat down on my couch. Then I noticed the bluebird had followed me, he flew to the window next to where I was sitting and stayed with me the whole day. Now it has been two years, and my little angel, the bluebird still comes and stays with me. Watching over me and letting me know that I am not alone. I feel like he is a gift from God. That little bird brings me peace, and when I see him, I am comforted. I have never seen a bluebird like this one in all the 14 years I have lived here in my house.

I was having a hard time in my life when I met him. Losing my mom and my dad really was taking a toll on me mentally and physically, but along came my little bluebird, and along came my peace. I know this is a gift, as both my mother and father had a love for birds, so what a better way to give me peace than to send my little blue angel to brighten my days. *God loves us so much.*

Our Lord gives us special gifts to help us get through the hard times, and whatever he uses to comfort us in our moments of affliction, well they are always just what we need. And mine was my little bluebird, and he was just what I needed...

In Loving Memory of my Parents- always and forever shining in my heart.

Scripture Share

"Come to me, all you who are weary and burdened, and I will give you rest.

Take my yoke upon you and learn from me, for I am gentle and humble in heart,

and you will find rest for your souls.

For my yoke is easy and my burden is light."

-(Matthew 11:28-30, NIV)

Forever Grateful, Colleen

> The LORD says, "I will guide you along the best pathway for your life. I will advise you and watch over you.
> -(Psalm 32:8, NLT)

Uncle Clay wrote to me,

Colleen explained the topic of your new book as having something to do with Angels or miracles or great things He has done. If I don't have that exactly correct, please forgive me. I am not sure my story qualifies for any of that but here it is. So April as you know, I was pretty heavily involved in arm wrestling. I am sure you heard many stories and probably actually may remember some of them. I know you were pretty young. So here goes. I will try not to get too far off track. I hope you find it interesting and hopefully useful for your purposes.

Thank you Uncle Clay and Aunt Colleen …for your willingness to share what the Lord can do…

THE WAY MAKER
Clay Rosencrans

So it is hard to know exactly where to start….

I started arm wrestling with my brothers and friends and anyone who was willing from about ten years old. My dad promoted competition among his sons. I had a brother Cliff a year older than me and a brother Cole a year younger than me.

My oldest brother Calvin was five years my senior. He brought friends home that I had to try and beat. I have to admit that I liked the attention, and I was full of myself and liked to show off. I was rebellious and cocky.

My father was domineering and abusive at times, but he was also a positive force in my development.

I cut school and ran with some troubled kids that could be bad influences. I was probably a bad influence on them as well. Needless to say, this led to some bad choices.

I did work hard as a kid in the family tree business and grew strong physically. I left home at 16 because of an unwillingness to take the abuse any longer from my father. I went right to work full-time as a shipping clerk in a warehouse. I tried to continue my high schooling part- time but that did not work out so well.

Eventually I got in trouble for growing weed and because it was a first offense, I was allowed to attend some drug counseling classes and not have it go on my permanent record. So the Counselor facilitating the classes made an impact on me as he complimented me on my athletic ability. During the 3-hour long classes held in a recreation building, there was a recess period. With a park outside and about 20 other guys in the class, we played football with the Counselor. Afterwards he pulled me to the side and asked me 'what I was doing wasting my *God- given* athletic abilities on weed, and why was I not pursuing a career in professional sports?'

This was one of the first of many wake- up calls for me. I began to look at myself differently from then on.

At the time, I had no idea how I could make use of my physical ability other than manual labor. One thing led to another and after a short time, I found myself competing at a high level in arm wrestling. This is how I met Colleen, (my future wife) your Dad and the rest of the Raney family. Things happen fast when you are 19 years old. In a short period of time through some unusual circumstances, I became aware of my need for my salvation, the reality of an all-powerful loving, perfect Heavenly Father.

I got married, had a baby daughter, and became a *multiple- time, World Champion arm wrestler.*

I met a lot of Christian arm wrestlers. One group of Christian arm wrestlers had a burden for Prison ministry. They asked me and another World Champion arm wrestler (My training partner Virgil Arcerio) (recently passed) if we would like to be involved in putting together some events at southern Ca. Prisons. We agreed and took an arm-wrestling table and the gospel message to Chino and Terminal Island Prisons. The events were well received, and many prisoners responded! Both to the arm wrestling and to the sharing of the Gospel. They appreciated the opportunity to get beat one after another as they stood in line while we took turns showing them the various techniques.

Somehow the 700 Club and Pat Robertson heard about what we were doing and invited us to be on the Christian Talk Show. They offered to fly us out there to Virginia Beach, Virginia, and talk about what we were doing. I was a self-employed Tree Maintenance Worker at the time, not making much money but was encouraged to go. So I went. It was a humbling experience. I felt somewhat unworthy of all that expense they were putting out, with the cost of the flight, the hotel, and other costs…

So the day of the departure, I drove our eight-year-old 72 Pinto station wagon to LAX. I did not quite make it all the way there. The car overheated. I had to park it and walk the last couple of miles or so.

It was an early Saturday morning flight and it seemed like I was not going to get there in time. I was very disappointed with myself as I had no extra money and no credit cards. I did not have enough money or time to call a cab. I was hoping someone might stop and pick me up as I was jogging down Century Blvd, with my thumb out. I remember there were a lot of shops that were not open because it was about 5:30 AM. As I made my way towards the Airport, I thought it odd that a man wearing a suit was just standing there in the middle of the sidewalk. He looked like a tall successful, middle-aged businessman and somewhat out of place. We made eye contact as I went past. After a few more steps I looked back to see if maybe he was getting into a car or something.

He was gone and there were no cars parked there. There was, however, a fifty-dollar bill where he had been standing. I stopped, went back, and picked up the money. I looked around; it was as though he had suddenly vanished. No open shop doors, nothing. I stood there for a few seconds scratching my head looking for anywhere he could possibly have gone. I did not have time to wait around.

As I started back towards the airport, I thought what anyone may have thought, maybe I had just seen an [11]Angel. Maybe God sent me that fifty.

My fears of missing the flight left me and somehow, I knew I was going to be on that jet. I did not know how, and time was not on my side for making it on foot. I began to look for taxicabs. Then all of a sudden, a car pulled up. It was one of the arm-wrestling Christians involved with the prison ministry. He was not going with us. He said he decided to come see us off at the airport and support what we were doing. I climbed in and away we went. It all happened so fast and with no time to spare. Elijah did not know

---

[11] Exodus 23:20,ESV-*"Behold, I send an angel before you to guard you on the way and to bring you to the place that I have prepared.*

of my car breaking down, he did not know to look for me walking....

I was a little bit stunned by the turn of events. I can't say for certain what happened there that day. I did get on that flight with two of my Christian arm-wrestling buddies and we were interviewed on the 700 Club. When We got back four days later Elijah greeted us and held up my keys and said he had put a new water pump and hose in, and the car was running fine and in the airport parking lot.

Divine Appointments Keep Coming
April Yarber-Berg

Divine appointments can start off one way and become another altogether. It all depends on how God delivers them.

> *The natural person does not accept the things of the spirit of God, for they are folly to him, and he is not able to understand them because they are spiritually discerned.*
>
> *- (1 Corinthians 2:14, ESV)*

How I met Jackie, Well, I haven't actually met her in person yet, just online during meetings we have for an online screenwriters group that we are both in. Jackie actually started the group. I had been daydreaming a lot about someone picking up one of my stories for a movie, and then one day out of nowhere Jackie decided to start a screenwriters group by posting something in the *CHS, Called Higher Studios, Facebook group. Of course, I was immediately like," I'm in." I have been wanting to learn to write a screenplay. So, I thought it would be good to join and learn from the others in the group, and develop my own screenplay along the way. So far, we have had more than a few meetings and it is wonderful. These people are absolutely, hands down some of the most beautiful, talented, souls I've ever met.

I am thoroughly convinced that God joined us all together for a reason greater than our own.

I'm also very grateful to Jackie for listening to her Holy Spirit and getting us all together. Below is the email from Jackie, who so graciously said I could use her God winks in the book…

Jackie wrote:

Yes, I've had a few supernatural experiences, but I think they're more like little winks from God. Anything more would maybe freak me out a bit… LOL (laugh out loud). God knows how to meet us where we're at!...

HE LIVES
Jackie Gebbia

Back in 2020 my mother had a major cardiac arrest while she was in the hospital. In a desperate attempt to reach her in time, my brother-in-law was driving behind the wheel, racing to get me there. I'll never forget the terror I was experiencing. All my senses were heightened to the point where I felt separated from my body. I couldn't think. I couldn't speak. My brain was on overdrive. Everything was moving in slow motion just like in the movies.

We approached a busy intersection and had to stop at a red light. I was so upset at the delay. But "something" made me turn my head toward the driver's side window. As if a hand gently nudged my face toward that direction. In the turning lane was a bright red convertible. I happened to glance down at the license plate. It read "HE LIVES."

Although I couldn't fully appreciate the experience until several weeks later, I knew it wasn't a coincidence. God was showing me that He was present. Even in the worst gut-wrenching moment of my life.

THE WHITE FEATHER
Jackie Gebbia

I never did make it on time as my mother went to the be with the Lord by the time we got there.

But in that same week while I was in prayer, I decided to speak to my mother. I asked her to give me a sign to let me know that she could hear me and that everything was okay. All I could think of for a sign was a simple white feather. For a few days I was actually looking out for it whenever I stepped outside. I had naturally assumed that's where I would find one.

A week went by and nothing. Then one day, my sister and I were in Marshall's looking for something to wear for the memorial service. I happened to pass by the shoe department and noticed a large display of Jessica Simpson shoes. On the cover of the boxes was a printing of a single white feather. At first It didn't register. Maybe because it wasn't where I thought a feather would appear. I caught up to my sister and casually mentioned it to her.

She immediately became excited and proclaimed, "That's it! That's it!" Of course that's the sign!" My sister reminded me how much my mother loved fashion and going shopping. It was from her! I just laughed. My mother was never the type to enjoy being outdoors in nature - where I assumed I would find the feather. But a clothing store? Absolutely! It made perfect sense!

HE HEARS YOU
Jackie Gebbia

I will aways treasure these little unexpected supernatural experiences. However, I have to admit there is one moment that still amazes me most. It happened around 2018 or 2019, before I had fully become a born-again Christian. For several months I had been actively pursuing God. Even though at the time it was considered more similar to practicing the law of attraction (LOA), I never once believed that I could do anything on my own without God. I knew that for certain. And it was the foundation I grew up on as a Catholic and never once strayed from. LOA was just a process to help me focus more on positive, uplifting thoughts. And it actually did help me get through a bout of depression.

But as I got deeper into the process and heard how other people were seeing God manifest their dreams, I was starting to have doubts. Doubting whether God even heard me or noticed me. I mean, there are 8.1 billion of us humans living in the world. God has a lot to deal with, right? All those billions of people. In the greater scheme of things, who am I to even get noticed? (Remember, this was BEFORE I became born again) So one day I was feeling pretty low due to these doubts. I had just left a local Home Depot and became irritated because they were out of something I had needed for my garden. My mind was just racing with negative thoughts. I wasn't really paying much attention to anything other than this constant chatter in my head. On my way back home, I pulled up behind an SUV that was stopped at a red light. (There's that red light again.) I happened to glance down at the license plate. It read "HI JACKIE." What??? Who would get a license plate like that? I leapt up in my seat and laughed in amazement. God is real! And He is with us all the time. Just like He says He is! So keep your eyes open because you never know what message He's trying to show you!

> *It is the glory of God to conceal things, but the glory of kings is to search things out.*
> *-(Proverbs 25:2, ESV)*

> *" The secret things belong to the Lord our God, but the things that are revealed belong to us and to our children forever, that we may do all the words of this law.*
> *-(Deuteronomy 29:29, ESV)*

> *Send out your light and your truth; let them lead me; let them bring me to your holy hill and to your dwelling!*
>
> *-(Psalm 43:3, ESV)*

I have a **question** for you...

Are you living as your best authentic self? Are you living as the person God says you are and whom he created you to be? Or are you unwittingly living your life based upon a lie? Perhaps it began as an unkind remark heard in childhood. A derogatory opinion about you that was expressed by a mother, father, sibling, teacher, classmate, or relative. Maybe someone else's fears and insecurities were slowly instilled in you over time, from an overprotective yet well- intentioned parent, and you unknowingly assumed this identity by slipping into it, as you would a familiar pair of comfortable old Nikes. What if you've been living your whole life under this false identity and you've been completely oblivious to it?

MY PERSONAL STORY TO SHARE ABOUT BULLYING

During my junior high and high school years I was the target of bullying. Every unkind word that was said to me I took to heart and accepted as fact. It got to the point where I eventually began to believe that I wasn't good enough, pretty enough, or worthy enough. Those years were supposed to be my time to shine. I was an honor student, I excelled in art and sports. I was like a sunflower ready to burst open and blossom. But instead, I shrunk back. Closed my petals and dimmed my own light so that I would in essence become invisible. Because when you're invisible, you no longer can be seen as an easy target. You're no longer seen at all. You just want to fade into the background and disappear. As I entered into adulthood, I thought I had moved past it. But every so often there were moments that triggered emotions of profound sadness. I was the walking wounded without any visible signs of my injury. I felt I was unlovable. How could anyone

love and accept me when I didn't even love and accept myself? I actually hated myself and often wondered, what is wrong with me? Why did I always feel like an outsider? A misfit? I knew I was intelligent and talented but why was life such a constant battle to feel comfortable in my own skin? A struggle, to fit in. I just wanted to be ordinary like everyone else.

Friendships came and went. Romantic relationships came and went. I was unconsciously self-sabotaging my relationships out of fear of being rejected again. I built a wall of protection around my heart and kept people at arm's length, so that no one could get too close and discover the "real me." But that "me" wasn't the real me at all anyway! It was a false identity I unknowingly assumed, by accepting everything negative that other people said about me. I experienced a few dark nights of the soul. Many times I thought I was down for the count. Yet despite it all, I never gave up. There was something deep within me that would not allow me to. No matter how deep and dark the pit was, I would always fight and claw my way back up to the surface again, in search of the light. Always the light.

After many years of continued ups and downs, I felt mentally and emotionally exhausted. I had been spinning my wheels looking for my purpose and place in the world, and not getting anywhere. Friends were all on track moving forward with their lives, and I felt like I was still standing at the starter's gate. I finally came to the conclusion that no amount of personal self-development books I had been devouring, no law of attraction courses, no ah-ha moments from Oprah, was going to fix me and completely transform my life. No one. Except Jesus.

In the Fall of 2018, I took a deep breath and repeated the prayer of Salvation. In my bedroom. In my pajamas, while listening to *Joyce Meyer reciting it on TV, I made the choice to surrender my life to Christ. SURRENDER. I want you to know how scary this concept is for a lifelong, self-professed control freak. I barely got the word out of my mouth. I've always believed in God. Always prayed. But surrendering my life? What exactly does that mean? What does it even look like? Would I have to get all religious now? Read the Bible 24/7 and cancel my subscription to HBO?

I had actually been on the precipice of making this commitment for quite a while before I finally decided to just let go and take a leap of faith. But the truth is, I literally did not see any other option. I wasn't getting any younger. I was tired of running (mainly from myself) I had nowhere left to turn. So I turned right into the arms of Jesus.

Ironically, and to my utter amazement, it was in my surrendering that I found FREEDOM. It had nothing to do with religion at all. But it had everything to do with having a personal and intimate relationship with Jesus. And as I started studying His Word, the negative beliefs I had about myself, eventually gave way to accepting what God says about me, According to God, I am...

LOVED

"In all these things we are more than conquerors through him who loved us. For I am convinced that neither death nor life, neither angels nor demons, neither the present nor the future, nor any powers, neither height nor depth, nor anything else in all creation, will be able to separate us from the love of God that is in Christ Jesus our Lord."
(Romans 8:37-39, NIV)

ACCEPTED

"The Lord your God is with you, the Mighty Warrior who saves. He will take great delight in you; in his love he will no longer rebuke you, but will rejoice over you with singing."
(Zephaniah 3:17, NIV)

WORTHY

"Since you are precious and honored in my sight, and because I love you, I will give people in exchange for you, nations in exchange for your life." (Isaiah 43:4, NIV)

CAPABLE

"But you shall remember the Lord your God, for it is He who is giving you power to make wealth, that He may confirm His covenant which He swore to your fathers, as it is this day." (Deuteronomy 8:18, NIV)

VALUABLE

"Look at the birds of the air; they do not sow or reap or store away in barns, and yet your heavenly Father feeds them. Are you not much more valuable than they?" (Matthew 6:26, NIV)

BLESSED

Every good gift and every perfect gift is from above, coming down from the Father of lights with whom there is no variation or shadow due to change. (James 1:17, NIV)

Encouragement

It was in my surrendering that I found acceptance.

It is in your surrender that you will find acceptance.

It was in my surrendering that I found wholeness.

It is in your surrender that you will find wholeness.

It was in my surrendering that I found peace.

It is in your surrender that you will find peace.

It was in my surrendering that I found the real ME.

It is in your surrender that you will DISCOVER the real YOU. And then you can finally become all God calls you to be.

Blessings. Jackie

> *But do not overlook this one fact, beloved,*
> *that with the Lord one day is as a thousand*
> *years, and a thousand years as one day.*
> *-(2 Peter 3:8, ESV)*

HIS PERFECT TIME
April Yarber -Berg

WAIT…Just when it's needed… God provides!

Sometimes things take longer than we hope for, and in these times, we are called to be patient. I know it can be unbearably hard sometimes-

To WAIT- to STOP- and to be STILL, but we need to remember- most things in life that are worth anything, require waiting. God's timing is always perfect. There is a song by 'Tom Petty' that sums it up pretty perfectly, and what is it called you ask? Like you can't guess, unless you aren't really a Tom Petty fan- Well it's called The Waiting- (Petty, 1981). In one of the main verses he sings, "The waiting is the hardest part. "And isn't that true? It absolutely is- the hardest part- and it usually comes after the other hardest part, which usually requires doing something. Like taking a leap of faith....

Hey, but aren't there any *easy parts*?

Thankfully, there are, it happens after the *action* of finally surrendering whatever we are doing to God. So now, the once impossible, well seems to become possible and it even seems to become better than the truth of our own imagined outcomes. It's *easier* when you learn to walk in God's will. It absolutely is easier than not. But another hard part is learning just what His Will looks like for your life. How can you align yourself with His Will? Well, you can start off by asking Him, and pray, my faith family, pray…also be patient. Remember a day is like a thousand years and a thousand years are like one day to God. So stay hopeful with faith forward, and do not lose heart. Have patience-knowing [12]God will always fulfill His promises right on time. (His perfect-perfect time.)

---

[12] Numbers 23:19, ESV *"God is not a man, that he might lie, or a son of man, that he might change his mind. Has He not said, and will He not do it? Or has he spoken, and will he not fulfill it?"*

I had put a post out on Facebook several times asking people if they would like to share their true stories/ God winks with me, and a whole year went by with no answer to the post, A whole year just flew by, but today I reposted and today someone replied. God knows just *who* to send and *when* to send them. Her name is Shannon, and her story is just what I needed to see.

There has also been a verse that has been popping up everywhere, it has been staring me in the face for more than a few days now. It is- from Proverbs.

> *A generous person will prosper; whoever refreshes others will be refreshed.*
> -(Proverbs 11:25, NIV)

Now I see where the verse fits in, it is completely in the timing because it seems so fitting for Shannon's story.

As always, April

✝

GODS GOT YOU COVERED
Shannon Lumley

I worked at a restaurant as a waitress, and regularly, earned tips. A lady who was a regular customer asked me, " What I would buy If I got a big tip?" I told her I would buy a new winter coat. That *same* day I got a $60 tip. I bought my winter coat. It was already winter and so, so cold.

Sometime later, I was putting my winter coat in the washing machine when my Mom asked, " Why I was washing it so soon after buying it." I told her I helped someone move and I got it all sweaty. After the wash it smelled nice and clean, it was back to good as new. Later that day I had to go somewhere. It was freezing outside and icy. I didn't like driving when the roads were icy, but I headed out.

When I was almost there, I saw a man in a T-shirt standing outside on the side of the road with a sign asking for money. He was jumping up and down just to keep warm. His face was purple from the cold. I didn't have any money, but I wanted to help him. So I handed the winter coat out the window to him. He thanked me and put it on right away.

It *fit* him *perfectly*.

When I got home my Dad said,' he had a Christmas present for me, and he wanted to give it to me early.' When I opened it, I couldn't believe my eyes, it was a winter *coat*! He could not have known at all what I had done.

Special dedication from Shannon to her dad…

Scripture Share

To the only God, our Savior, through Jesus Christ our Lord, be glory, majesty, dominion, and authority before all time now and forever. Amen - (Jude 1:25, ESV)

Shannon

Faithful is the LORD Fear Not
April Yarber

I believe most of us, if not all of us, have at one time or another experienced fear in the dark.

Sometimes we may even experience the opposite of the calm glowing light of the Lord. Sometimes we may even feel threatened in our spirit, by some-thing, or someone unseen… it might even be a place that may give us a shiver or a chill, that horrible warning that sets off deep inside us as an unsettling feeling takes over. During these times hopefully we aren't too afraid to ask God for protection. Thankfully, my friend wasn't too afraid to seek God for help. And God provided what she asked, and in the process, He allowed her a glimpse beyond the veil…

It's amazing to think about, but hard to truly fathom for us humans. Although we know in our hearts that God exists, it seems a bit more difficult to imagine that angels and demons also exist.

They aren't just found in movies, but they are found throughout history, within the pages of the BIBLE and are still found today in personal experiences' all over the globe. In fact from time to time, they are still experienced and shared in this present life. By someone you may know, perhaps even you. Fanning your faith from flicker to FLAME.

> *Of the angels he says, "He makes his angels winds, and his ministers a flame of fire."*
> *-(Hebrews 1:7, ESV)*

So, when you hear people speak of angels, just know that they are really HUGE, at least this is what I hear from those who have been blessed enough to have witnessed them up close.

> *But the Lord is faithful. He will establish you and guard you against the evil one.*
> *-(2 Thessalonian 3:3, ESV)*

✝

ANGELS STANDING GUARD
Monica Ayala

My story begins when I was on my way to work one morning, and as usual, I'm always forgetting something. It was no surprise, I did!! It had been my PHONE!

Running late, I decided to turn back! Ran inside and went straight to my son's room because we shared the restroom since we lived in a one-bedroom apartment.

But before all this happened, I previously had been feeling bad spiritual entities coming from my son's room! Scary? Yes, a little frightening, but God's Presence was with me every step of the way. He had reassured for me not to be afraid, for I AM with you! I can't explain it, but these entities felt like they really wanted to place harm to my son.

So whenever I would hear noises coming from the room, inside the closet, I would have the courage to go and face what the enemy had to bring. I know we cannot overcome the devil, but God can! Amen! So I'd run, turn on the light from the closet run out bend over my son's bed on one knee; place my bible on the bed and start residing scripture!

I had been praying for protection that God would send a host *ministering angels* to come to protect my son from any harm. So that one Monday morning, He did just that!.

As I ran in, I slowly opened the door and to my surprise!!! I've never seen anything like it, I saw two huge angels, like giants I've never seen before! Just standing still, as I opened the door the one on the left turned his head and his wings opened up like in attack mode; the second one on the right kept guard facing the window never moved. They both had their arms crossed like an "X" formation, but when the one on the left that stood on one side of my son's bed while sleeping; I think realized who I was at that moment and that's when his wings went down.

The angel of the Lord encamps around those who fear Him, and delivers them.
-(Psalm 34:7, ESV)

I call them he, because they were a form of a man, but no gender and faces of an eagle, hair full of crystal so heavy looking and very loud with a swishing sound! Their wings were huge silver in color and looked heavy enough to bring a whole wall down. These angels were a bluish gray color with broad shoulders very strong looking; masculine!! But very beautiful beings! I was startled at first, but realize spiritually that God had sent these beautiful beings for the protection of my son. There must been something huge for God to have sent them.. Did I remember my phone?? At that moment, nothing in this world mattered! Knowing that God does hear our prayers...Until this day, It is something so amazing about this that I will always cherish in my life as a faithful Godly women of Christ.

Scripture Share

Therefore let anyone who thinks
he stands take heed lest he fall
  -(1 Corinthians 10:12, NKJ)

Encouragement

We all go through hardships, but we don't have to go it alone! [13]God sent His only begotten Son, to save us from our sins and deliver us into the hands of God. He gives us the opportunity to get to know Jesus through the Gospels and for the unbelievers, doubters, and scoffers, miracles were performed to show others that Jesus *is* the Messiah. To those who are without family, He lets us know that He is our family. He is our Father: and that we are never alone. When we are without-He provides! When we feel unloved-He shows us His love and fills us with joy, but we *must* seek Him *diligently* Amen.

God Bless you always love. Monica

---

[13] John 3:16,ESV- *For God so loved the world, that he gave his only Son, that whoever believes in him should not perish but have eternal life.*

Be Patient His Timing is Everything

Answered prayers are wonderful and most likely completely answered differently than you had imagined. The prayer itself being answered may be in fact exactly what you asked for, but sometimes the package that it gets delivered in is what can be surprising. But hey, what do you expect when your prayer is for a companion, to find the love of another human being. Don't forget, they have prayers too. And isn't it sweeter still when you find out they are *ready* for your love and that they have also been asking God for you too?

God is so, so, *good*. Believe it and trust Him. His timing is everything….

ANSWERED PRAYERS
April Yarber- Berg

Just a little more about the miraculous things God can and does do, He most definitely answers our heart's prayers. I had prayed and asked God to send me a partner, just like many ladies do, a perfect guy to call my own, I had waited for the perfect match to appear. As a single mom, it seemed like years were flying by. I dated on and off and must admit I cried a lot and was disappointed even more than that.

Although I never *stopped* hoping. Dating isn't anything I miss.

By the way, my hats off to you single people, I know first-hand what being single is like, and well for most people it isn't easy. At least not for a single person who doesn't want to be single.

Someone once told me (*long ago*) that in my prayer life when talking to God I should be very specific. So, I took the time and made a list of relational qualities and physical attributes that I wanted my dream husband to possess. I read it aloud to God and put it away in my desk and forgot all about it. (*It was in there for about 2 years people*).

Then one day I met my husband. After I met James, I accidentally pulled out that list that I had made as a request to God.

I was looking for another item in my desk and as I drew my hand back, out came a tattered- looking piece of paper. It fell to the floor I reached down to pick it up and unfolded it, a quiet smile of amusement crossed my face. 'That's odd, should I read it?' I thought… The timing was an unspoken hint from God, and I knew as I began reading, well my description to God, how so ever uncanny, was and is, a perfect description of my now- husband- James.

God at the time, definitely answered almost all my checks on the list. However, a few of them well would be answered later, after James sobriety. Looking back at the list (which I have saved for posterity) It is like I described James flawlessly and perfectly without ever knowing him, but that's just another example of how God works. He answers our prayers in His time and with his beautiful provisions. How grateful we should be always…

OUR FIRST MEETING

I met James during the afternoon on a Sunday near my house, at a place down by the beach, it is a little rooftop restaurant and bar. My friend Lauren and I went to have sushi for lunch and then decided to walk over to the rooftop bar to check it out.

As soon as we walked in, I can recall walking right back outside to an empty table on the patio. Walking towards the table, we passed three guys that were talking to each other. I noticed briefly that one of them, in particular, was looking our way. I heard him say to his friends, "I want to stand by her." They then began walking over to us and parked themselves next to us at the table. While introducing themselves they added, "Do you mind if we sit here? I don't know which one did the introduction, I just remember their names, because I found it amusing. Their names are James #1, James #2, and Matt, and I thought it was so funny, (the two James), it reminded me of a sitcom I had seen that had 3 brothers named Daryl in it. I still find it funny.

Anyways back to my babe, a little while after that, James and I started dating. We had been dating for a few months. We were both drinking a lot, in fact, he was an alcoholic. I knew in my heart that I didn't want to continue living this way and I thought about my children. Especially my youngest Autumn. So, every morning on my way to work I would talk to God, asking Him to watch over my children, and my loved ones, and I would always close with an additional prayer:

"Lord, if this isn't the man for me remove him, but if he is, then clean him up, I know you don't want me to be with an alcoholic and that you don't want me to become an alcoholic, so if he is to be my husband... show me!"

I never told James about that prayer until after God began to move...

WHEN YOU WITNESS GOD MOVING IT IS TRULY AMAZING-

One night Lauren, James, and I were sitting in my garage, and out of nowhere, James says, "I want to go to rehab." Within 2 days, he called his aunt, and off he went to Prescott, Arizona. He was gone for 3 months. It was really hard for me, I was struggling to keep my faith, because of what I knew to be my prayer to the Lord.

And how I saw God answering, remembering the list I'd made about my perfect partner knowing it was my babe. But I still questioned… Over and over many times over those 3 months, I wrestled with the thoughts of unbelief, not knowing if James would truly come back to me. I am after all, only human. We all have doubts- even when we see God working in front of our eyes. (Oh, ye of little faith.)

During James's three months away at the rehab, another small desire of mine came true. Because we couldn't talk on the phone, we were forced to use the age-old way of communication-writing letters and mailing them by way of the United States Post Office, also known as snail mail... It was a little bit of excitement each time I went to the mailbox to see if I had received anything from James. And when I did, it was better than I had imagined.

I had received several beautiful love letters from him, ones just like you see in the movies. It was a fulfillment of a once young girl's fantasies and brought happiness to my heart (and still does). He wrote some beautiful words to cherish. Tangible letters, that I could hold onto, look back at, and share with my daughters and grandchildren someday.

Anyways thank God that James came back to me, and we both have been sober for 8 years. When he came back, he had told me a story of something that happened to him. Something that confirms to James and me, that God has everything to do with his successful sobriety. And in our heart of hearts, we *know* that it was the [14]*Lord* who paired us together. He walks with us in the union of our relationship, and the journey of our love. Making us stronger than we could ever be on our own. We both know that this beautiful life we now have together is definitely all God, and we thank Him for it. We actually got married in December, on 12/22 (remember my favorite number sequence- 222).

My *husband* James...

Matthew 19:4-6,ESV-[14] *He answered, "Have you not read that he who created them from the beginning made them male and female, and said, 'Therefore a man shall leave his father and his mother and hold fast to his wife, and the two shall become one flesh'? So they are no longer two but one flesh. What therefore God has joined together, let not man separate."*

Oh, sounds so wonderful to finally say that. Like I was saying before he had shared with me a true story of an amazing thing that had happened to him at the rehab. And he has agreed to share it in this book.

Thank you, honey. I love you…

Shortly after arriving at the rehab, James fell into the routine of his program. They had different classes and activities to attend all day long, some of which included AA meetings, yoga, camping, counseling, and breath- work. If you don't understand what breath-work is, well it is a form of meditation using deep breathing exercises. During His breath-work class is where he had the experience.

> *And it is my prayer that your love may abound more and more, with knowledge and all discernment.*
> *-(Philippians 1:9, ESV)*

FOCUS ON HIM
James Berg

One of my roommates at the rehab had mentioned to me that he really liked this breath-work class and that I should try it. So, I signed up.

When I got to the class, we had to lay on the ground with our backs on these pillows that were set up all around us. Then the instructor started telling us to take large deep breaths in and out. While I was doing the breathing my arms and my mouth tightened up, then I started to go into a dream state.

In the distance, I could visibly see my mom Cathy, who had passed away about a year and a half before this. I wanted so bad to see her clearly. I was trying so hard to focus on her, trying to get her attention, but she *wouldn't* let me. She kept motioning and directing my attention to the Presence on my left. Which was an overwhelming sensation of the Lord's Presence, helping me to realize that He has been with me all along. All the horrible things I had gone through in my life, even all the times I doubted Him, God was *with* me all along.

My mom didn't want me to focus on her. She wanted me to stay focused on the Lord because she knew He is what I needed to take care of me and get sober. I literally started to bawl like a baby.

And then I could feel the instructor put her hand on me and I was pulled out of the dream state.

The meaning to me is; keep *your focus* on *HIM*.

I felt so lost- throughout my life and had no trust in the Lord, because of the troubles of my past, and I was using my alcoholism to cope, to somehow fill a void. Now looking back through sober eyes, I can finally acknowledge without a doubt that I know " God has not only changed my life, but he has *saved* my life, and was with me through all of it. Today, I am right where I need to be- focused on Him and thankful.

I'm grateful to Him for my sobriety and for the life I live today. I know my momma would be proud of the man I've become.

Special thanks to my momma, for showing me the way!

    I love you- Bigger than the Sky Bigger than the Universe.
                      (BTTSBTTU)

Encouragement

No matter how alone you feel. He is with you and will never leave your side. And just like my momma pointed out ' He's been with you all along....

Love -James

25 "All this I have spoken while still with you. 26 But the Advocate, the Holy Spirit, whom the Father will send in my name, will teach you all things and will remind you of everything I have said to you. 27 Peace I leave with you; my peace I give you. I do not give to you as the world gives. Do not let your hearts be troubled and do not be afraid.

- (John 14:25-27, NIV)

In Loving Memory of my Beautiful Momma Cathy Hall

So we fix our eyes not on what is seen, but on what is unseen, since what is seen is temporary, but what is unseen is eternal.
-(2 Corinthians 4:18, NIV)

BEAUTIFUL LILY AT THE BANQUET TABLE
Debbie Golceker

I wanted to tell you how I'm feeling this Thanksgiving…

My family has experienced great loss over the last six years with the passing of my mom, brother, sister and recently my dad. They were all very painful but for some reason Thanksgiving always brings my heart back to my sister Cathy. My other sister Pat described it best when she went to the ocean near where my sister's ashes are spread with two lilies (Cathy's favorite). She threw them in the ocean. One was beaten and thrashed by the waves and torn apart. The other remained untouched and *beautiful* and rode peacefully on the waves. That best describes Cathy. This world was very tough for her and tried it's best to destroy her, but my wonderful, brave, amazing sister decided with the help of the *Lord* to reach out and change that.

We all got one year of Cathy that I will always be grateful for.

She had the most tender heart of anyone I have ever known, and we got to become best friends again for that year.

For those of you who have suffered the loss of a loved one you know there are those times that just hit you and Thanksgiving is that day for me. My sister never missed a Thanksgiving at our house. She took the bus everywhere for the last twenty or so years of her life, but on this day I got to pick her up from her weekly, with her HUGE Tupperware in hand and bring her over for dinner. My sisters and myself love the skin of the turkey (I know the worst part for you) and Cathy would always sneak behind my back and after I took it out of the oven she would take as much skin as she could. Isn't it crazy the silly things you miss? Then when dinner was over, and we hung out she would fill her Tupperware to the brim and have this indescribable smile on her face like a child at Christmas knowing she had left overs to bring home.

Now my sister is the other Lilly, peaceful, whole and sitting at the *ultimate banquet table.*

Scripture Share

²⁷ *"Look at the lilies and how they grow. They don't work or make their clothing, yet Solomon in all his glory was not dressed as beautifully as they are.*

²⁸ *And if God cares so wonderfully for flowers that are here today and thrown into the fire tomorrow, he will certainly care for you. Why do you have so little faith?* ²⁹ *"And don't be concerned about what to eat and what to drink. Don't worry about such things.*

-(Luke 12:27-29, NLT)

Encouragement

If there are those in your life that are being beat up by this world, hold them, hug them and love them. My sister, who lived in a weekly, rode a bus to wherever she had to go and had very few earthly possessions taught me invaluable lessons. Jesus has shown me through this that even if we feel that this world is wearing us down there is ALWAYS hope. My sister by the world's standards was not a stand out but in the eyes of the Lord she was/is His lily. Lily in Greek (souson) means beautiful flower. Mentioned many times in the Bible, the white lily symbolizes purity, rebirth, new beginnings and hope.

I love you Cathy and miss you with all my heart.

His Faithfulness-Debi

April's Journal entry 3/24/2021…

CONSIDER IT PURE JOY WHEN YOU SUFFER TRIALS OF MANY KINDS

Several Days of exhaustion -stuck in the muck and the mire. Knowing deep down if I can just muster up the strength to cry out to the Lord, He would hear me, save me, and help me. I just need some faith.

Feeling emotionally drained, bluer than blue. Hopeless, eyes swollen from crying and an emptiness trying to take hold of me. I cling tightly to my Lord, or as tightly as I can. For several days now I have been experiencing the lowest of emotions. Lying in bed, crying with a heavy feeling of hopelessness with no known reason behind it, this lowness I haven't experienced for a very long time. Feeling so low almost like a puddle of water seeping deep into the ground. Having worries, yet no energy to worry, anxieties and nightmares. Nightmares of war waged against God's people by evil. A stronghold of the enemy, trying to drain the light from within me.

I am feeling overwhelmed and weak these current days. In which I have little to no fight left. These times are so hard because you know that He is with you, but you cannot feel His Presence, and He seems so far away....

But my heart knows the truth... He, the Holy Spirit, is *here*. Just maybe there is something I'm missing. Something that I must do, that's why the enemy is throwing his all at me, and this may be why the Lord is allowing it. He is making me slow way down. I'm so puzzled though, as to what I am to do?...

And just a little while later same day that I wrote the entry above, something *amazing* happened...

The Lord's timing never ceases to amaze me. Just when I am feeling lost and frozen in place. Having no words- feeling void of direction -unknowing of what my next steps should be. He awakens my heart pulling that flickering faith to full flame, all by His timing of things delivered to me, by other believers. He restores us yes, often times using others to re-kindle the fires of faith and fan the flames. The timing of this story from Joy (which is needed so much right now) couldn't be more perfect.

Just as I'm feeling low crying out to the Lord, asking HIM what I should be doing, and telling Him how hopeless and lost I feel

because I don't know what he wants me to do !-

Joy's story came over via email out of the blue. A ping noise stopped me in my prayers, and I glanced at my iPhone where the notification briefly showed up on my screen, it read "*Having Faith.*"

This beautiful, shared God wink delivered at any other planned or expected time, well it would lose somehow the spiritual power to push me and encourage me into completing this book…

And without faith it is impossible to please Him, for whoever would draw near to God must believe that He exists and that He rewards those who seek Him.

(Matthew 21:22, ESV)

God knows what I so need to enable me to keep going. HE knows me full well. Just as He knows *you*. He knows just what we need and when it is needed most. So now I know, I am to finally sit down and finish this book with Faith Forward-

And Jesus said to him, "Go your way; your faith has made you well. "And immediately he recovered his sight and followed him on the way.

-(Mark 10:52, ESV)

✝

HAVING FAITH
Joy Ingram Grabarkewitz

On March 7th, 2013, we were headed to my Son's graduation from boot camp. As I shut the front door, I had an unsettling thought, the same thought I had over the last few days. I had a feeling something was going to happen; I didn't know what it was, just a feeling that I might not be coming home. I didn't think much about it, as the thought left my mind as quickly as it came.

The following day, we headed for home, and it wasn't until I saw our exit sign. I was maybe five minutes from home, when I had that same unsettling thought again. I remember thinking I wasn't sure why I was having these thoughts, as I was too close to home for something to happen.

I was *wrong*!

As we approached the top of the off-ramp, we slightly fish tailed. It had rained earlier that day and the road was slick, it didn't seem to matter that we were going slow. Our tire barely bumped the small curb when my Dad, who was with us said, "Are we going to roll?" The truck rolled three times before coming to a stop. My husband, dad, and brother were able to walk away, I wasn't so lucky.

To make a long story short, I spent ten hours in surgery, had multiple injuries, and five blood transfusions.

Three days later, I was still bleeding internally, and little did I know that I was about to take the ride of my life, I didn't know that I was headed back into surgery. I'm sure the doctors thought I was out before they started working on me, but I wasn't. I felt the scapple going into my leg. I found myself screaming to God, for help! I was so busy talking to God. I didn't see him, nor did I hear him, but as soon as I mentioned his Son,

I found myself sitting on a boat as old as time and I had this feeling of a Spirit next to me…

The water was like glass and in front of me, stood *Jesus*. I only saw him from the waist down, a gown, sandals, and hands, I knew it was Jesus! I thought I had faith, but he said I had little faith and at that moment, I knew that the spirit next to me was Peter.[15] Jesus spoke those same words to him. Our faith is so small compared to Jesus, yet so powerful.

Blessings, Joy

---

[15] Matthew 14:29-31, NIV *"Come, "he said. Then Peter got down out of the boat, walked on the water and came toward Jesus. But when he saw the wind, he was afraid and ,beginning to sink, cried out, "Lord save me! "Immediately Jesus reached out His hand and caught him. "You of little faith," He said, "Why did you doubt?"*

The Divine Appointment Via Facetime
April Yarber-Berg

Even after experiencing all the wonderous things the Lord has done in my life thus far, and even after hearing all the amazing true stories about His Divine interventions... I still get blown away when I see the map of His provision opening up before me, leading me.

As with an arrow onto a path, and at its point in front of me stands... His open door.

It's extraordinary the way He has certain events happen in order to unfold His Divine appointments, it reminds me that He is Omniscient and that we are always living in the Presence of God. That *knowing* gives me a sense of deep peace that only He can give and leaves me in relaxed gratitude. I can surrender my worries, knowing that everything is in His great hands.(As in these moments I can see it, His Will.)

I had thought I was just about ready to publish and be done with this book, but God has other plans for me... and He doesn't hold back. It will be done after every story He has meant for the book is available and delivered-right on time.

It was a Wednesday, and I was at work as usual...

I had only been there for about 2 hours when it was obvious to myself, and my boss, that I just wasn't feeling right. So she suggested I should go to my doctor's. Long story short, I am off work for the rest of the month. I left work that day early and stopped to get an afternoon coffee. I was talking to one of my aunts on the phone when all of a sudden, my phone went cuckoo, and it began face-timing someone named Agnes.

Honestly, it took me a moment before I realized it was this sweet lady named Agnes that I met at a bible study about 2 years earlier, who I might add, I had never talked to on the phone before. We only emailed a few times back and forth...I stood outside the coffee shop looking at my phone wondering, am I going to bother her? Should I hang up? But I had a feeling there was a reason that this was happening, so I just let it ring., and Agnes answered. There she was, I could see her kind face on my phone. We began laughing as I explained how by accident, oops, I mean (purpose- driven, Divine intervention) my phone had butt-dialed /face-timed her, calling her out of the blue. It was so nice to see her…

I told her maybe the Lord wanted me to pray for her, and that's why my phone called. She asked me how I was doing and then I told her that I was finally finishing my second book. She remembered me talking about it at the bible study so very long ago and asked if it was the book of testimonies? I explained it was more like people's true moments where they had very strong encounters with God, like God winks, stories of angels and other divine-type appointments. Immediately she said, "that's very interesting, I actually have had three very powerful experiences to share in the book."

I smiled and looked up. "Isn't that just so Jesus? "I said, this is so profound. No way I could make this stuff up?"

Agnes and I were both in awe of how Jesus worked out both our schedules so that we could have this divine appointment. She shared her stories with me, and I could see that they were so *perfect* for this book. All I can say is thank you Lord for your provision.

> *Praise the LORD, you His angels, you mighty ones who do his bidding, who obey his word. Praise the LORD, all his heavenly hosts, you his servants who do his will. Praise the LORD, all his works everywhere in his dominion. Praise the LORD, my soul*
>
> *-(Psalm 103:20-22, NIV)*

☦

THE EARTH ANGEL
Agnes Higginbotham

It was in November of 2008. I was on my way to buy some new shoes for my son's wedding in December.

When I arrived at the mall, I was going down the stairs to go inside one of the large department stores and misjudged the last step. As I slipped and fell, for a split second, it felt as if something or someone lifted me up so that I fell down gently. I fell right by a bench where a woman was sitting. She moved me against the nearby wall and said she was a nurse, and would I mind if she checked my legs. I felt so fortunate that someone so thoughtful was there to help since I was there alone. She examined my ankles and said she would stay with me until the store manager called the EMTs.

When the store manager came out and said an ambulance was on the way; I turned around to tell the nurse thank you and she was gone just that quick… The fall could have been a lot worse but as a result of the gentle fall, I broke my left ankle and sprained my right ankle instead of falling on my elbows. I call the nurse that helped me that day, my earth angel.

For it is written, "'He will command his angels concerning you, to guard you,'
-(Luke 4:10, ESV)

Whoever pursues righteousness and kindness will find life, righteousness, and honor.
-(Proverbs 21:21, ESV)

THE VISITING ANGEL
Agnes Higginbotham

Here's my second experience about two weeks after my mom passed away.

My mom, Katie, was a sweet, nurturing, and loving mother. She came to live with my husband and I after she suffered a stroke. My mom was with us here in California for seven years before she passed away from an abdominal aneurysm.

One day about two weeks after my mom passed, I came home from work and as I parked the car in the driveway a man came up behind me and said "excuse me, can you tell me where Albatross St. is in the neighborhood. " He had a very strong European accent (my mother was German, and she also had a strong German accent.) That's why I really felt strange, yet I didn't feel frightened. He had this very peaceful demeanor and the bluest eyes I've ever seen. He said he was jogging and didn't know how to get out of the cul-de-sac which I thought strange since he was jogging and had to come in the neighborhood in some manner.

After I told him where I thought the street, he was looking for might be. He said," thanks," and started to head in that direction I told him about how to get out of the cul-de-sac. I bent down for a few seconds to get my purse out of the car and turned back around to make sure he was heading in the right direction.

When I looked up, he was gone. I thought to myself, how could he have gotten to the street that fast? I was so stunned!

I looked in both directions and then ran into the house to ask my son if he heard me talking to a man (just to confirm what I just experienced) My son said, " yes, I heard him, what did he want?" I told my son that he just wanted to know where a certain street might be because he was lost and didn't know how to find his way out of the neighborhood. But he must have been a very fast jogger because when I turned around, and only after a few seconds, he had just disappeared. I feel that experience was my mom's spirit or a visiting angel trying to find their way home, and it was God's way of providing me a sense of peace since my husband and I were in deep mourning from our loss.

Here's the last experience I wanted to share…It happened about 20 years ago when my youngest son got into a little trouble….

THE ANGEL OF COMFORT
Agnes Higginbotham

I went to pick my son up from the HB civic center courthouse. I was very distraught and saddened by the path my son had taken.

As I waited outside for him to be released, a young man about the age of my son came up behind me and said, "Excuse me, I'm sorry for what you're going through, but don't worry everything will be okay. "I didn't feel frightened or apprehensive when he asked me to come sit down on a near bench. As we sat down a sense of peace came upon me. The young man said," I know your pain and hurt but don't worry, things will work out. Trust me because I've been there." All I could say was "I sure hope so" and thanked him for being so kind. I was puzzled and I wondered how he knew what I was going through?

I never told him about my son being in trouble.

As I was looking down, I looked up briefly and saw him get up to walk away, but in a few seconds, he was gone. It was a very strange yet comforting feeling that I experienced that day, which helped me get through the sadness…

I feel that young man was an *angel of comfort*, sent by the Lord just when I needed him most.

God Bless-Agnes

> *I will rejoice and be glad in your steadfast love,*
> *because you have seen my affliction;*
> *you have known the distress of my soul,*
> *-(Psalm 31:7, ESV)*

And God is able to make all grace abound to you, so having all sufficiency in all things at all times, you may abound in every good work.

(2 Corinthians 9:8, ESV)

April continues-

HE CALLS US- FOR HIS GLORY, TO BE TRANSPARENT AND HONEST SHARING WITH OTHERS THE JOYS OF OUR EXPERIENCES AND TESTIMONIES TO SHARE THE PURPOSES THAT ARE REVEALED TO US IN HIS DIVINE NATURE, AND WE ARE CALLED ALSO TO SHARE THE THINGS THAT ARE HARD FOR US TO BEAR.

[16]No matter what the circumstance, God will bring something good out of it.

☦

---

[16] ROMANS 8:28, ESV- *and we know that for those who love God all things work together for good, for those who are called according to his purpose.*

AWAKENING DESIRE
Nicole Gardner

I have met many people that love Jesus yet say they don't "hear" from God. I would have to back up and tell you how I came to surrendering my life to Jesus.

I grew up in an atheist home.

My parents were divorced, and my mom was an atheist. I was told my whole life that there was no God or devil, and we just live this life- then get buried and that's it.

The night of July 1, 2010, after I had put my kids to bed, I sat on my bedroom floor weeping with my .38 in my hand at the point of just taking my life. The devil was saying things like I'm a terrible mom, all I've done is screw up their life and everyone would be better off without me. Mind you it sounded very much like my own thoughts. (I know better now)

I'm not sure what it was I can only assume the Holy Spirit intervened on what I was about to do. I lifted my head and said out loud "okay God, if you want this life, You can have it, I've done nothing but screw it up." All I know is after that I was able to get up off the floor and go to bed.

The next morning I had a burning desire to know this *Jesus*.

I didn't own a bible, nor did I know anything about being a Christian, but I did wake up different and The Lord just started speaking to me. [17]I *knew* His voice. I think one main reason was that I didn't have any religion in my head to tell me otherwise. I know a lot of people that have had to unlearn and repent of wrong mindsets because of the denomination or the man rules that were taught to them growing up.

---

[17] John 10:27-30, ESV- *My sheep hear my voice, and I know them, and they follow me. I give them eternal life, and they will never perish, and no one is able to snatch them out of my hand. My Father who has given them to me, is greater than all, and no one is able to snatch them out of the Father's hand. I and the Father are one."*

THE FIRST ASSIGNMENT
Nicole Gardner

I thought I would share my first assignment from the Lord. I turned my life over to Jesus on July 10, 2010.

My husband and I were separated at the time. I was only working a small part-time job on the weekend. No money to speak of and scared to death how I was going to support myself and 3 kids and keep homeschooling them.

I was driving to the church I was attending at the time. I missed my freeway exit and ended up turning around in downtown Houston in a pretty bad area. I was a little panicked trying to figure out how to get to where I needed to be. I was at a stoplight and looked over and saw a group of homeless people hanging out or camped out. The Lord said, "take care of those people." I said what? And He told me again to take care of them. I thought 'what do you mean and how am I going to do that?'

One thing I do know how to do, and love doing, is cooking. I made the decision to bring them some food.

The next Sunday I make a bunch of breakfast tacos and snacks and juice and put them in individual bags. I drove to the same spot and pulled over to the curb. As if they were waiting for me, two men came over and took the bags from me. I did that for a couple of more weeks and then one morning the Lord said," I want you to get out." I was like, get out… Get out and do what? He said, 'Just get out and tell them your story.' Mind you I am only a few weeks old in the Lord and know little to nothing about the Bible or anything else other than the voice of the Lord.

I did get out and share my story, and for a few months took care of those people with a weekly meal, some clothes and a clothes and a couple of other things. I never gave them any money and they never asked me for any.

The point of the story is that if you want to help people, but you are waiting to get yourself together, you may be doing it *wrong*. Just listen; the Lord will give you someone or several someone's you can start helping now. In the end my husband came to Christ, we reconciled our marriage, the homeless camp got shut down and I never saw that particular group again. I one-hundred percent believe helping them was more to get my mind off myself and everything I was going through and focus on those that were way worse off than me.

It was the sweetest few months that got me through a horrible time in my life. …

A SINGLE ROSE
Nicole Gardner

On Mother's Day weekend back in 2019, I had attended a worship service with my husband, my mom, my two youngest kids, and my three grandchildren.

I usually would sit and worship up front of the church, but today, the Lord had told me to go to the back. I went to the back leaving my family up front and closed my eyes. When I opened my eyes, I saw a vision of my son Joshua standing in front of me, holding a single red rose.

This amazing vision from God was given to me on my first Mother's day since *losing* my son.

I loved seeing my son, but I wondered why a rose, why would he be giving me a rose? I wasn't the kind of lady who ever really liked flowers. Some ladies love flowers, but that wasn't me. So although I was filled with overwhelming joy seeing my son, I was still a little puzzled. The vision was so beautiful, but it faded away,

I wish I could have seen him longer. I went back up to the front and sat down with my husband.

After church was over, we were told that another mom and her daughter wanted to do something special for everyone in the church, so we stayed seated. Three dads came out holding their little ones and the kids were holding big heart cutouts and when they flipped them, they each said something on them, like my mom and you're so special.' It was so cute to watch, then the older kids came out...

all of them were holding *one single rose*...

Encouragement

I hope this helps, and I declare open ears and eyes for you, that you will come into a fullness of "knowing" the Godhead, Father, Son, and Holy Spirit that They may direct your every step! In the mighty name of Jesus Amen!!

Nicole

IMPENETRABLE PEACE
April Yarber-Berg

God gives us comfort from heaven, allowing us to see His mercies and with them they bring such a deep impenetrable PEACE.

Today is May 03, 2021. This day may not be significant to many people, but to my family it is. I will tell you why shortly…

Today, as I came out of the grocery store and entered my car to go home. I glanced down and I discovered a little red heart-shaped button on the passenger seat of my car. I thought it was odd as I hadn't noticed it before I had gone into the store, but there it was just sitting there on my passenger seat- smiling at me.

Let me back up a bit, and then it seems that I will have to back up even more so that you can get the full scope. The heart shape itself has a special meaning to me, as I recall beginning to notice them more predominantly a few years back.

They began standing out to me more and more frequently in the year 2010. I noticed I began seeing them a lot.

I didn't really understand at first why they would jump out at me. It could be a heart shaped cloud that I noticed, or a leaf, a rock, a puddle of water… or just anything shaped like a heart that stood out to me. As if it was waiting for me to discover it. The more I'd see them the more I began to realize just who was sending them. At first to be honest I felt like my cousin Stacey was saying" Hi" from heaven, but then, that 'God is ever so close feeling" began to become more prevalent, so whenever I would see them, I knew it to be something special from God.

At times He uses them to encourage me like saying,' you're on the right track.' Sometimes it's just to remind me that I am not alone, and not to give up. Other times I believe He uses them to comfort me. Whatever the case, whatever I'm feeling and whenever I see them, I see an indication of HIS love and feel His Presence strongly around me. I think of these little amazing moments like a secret conversation between HIM and I. Some people call them God winks, which is such a great description. This day having found the heart button on my seat I felt happy and loved and felt a confirmation that I was right where I needed to be. Looking up briefly I thanked God for my little love message. I then picked it up and studied it for a moment trying to find the place where it could have come from? Nothing rang a bell. I tried to think really hard, maybe it fell off some clothing I owned, but it was a red heart button, and I didn't own anything that had a button like that. So, I placed it back in the seat and drove home.

After I parked, before I went into my house, I sat in my car awhile and picked up the button again, this time I seemed to remember something familiar about it. As I turned it over, I noticed dry glue on one side. That's when it hit me, this button was glued on a ribbon that my daughter Amanda had made in honor of my cousin Stacey. So, this is where I'll back up even more. My cousin Stacey was murdered back in May of 1990.

Her murderer had finally been identified by DNA in 2010 (20 years after her murder), and it was the very year I began noticing hearts.

For all those years not knowing who took Stacey's life, was so hard, especially in the beginning, my family speculated and struggled, and many parts of our family crumbled, a lot of us fell apart for quite some time...

But thanks to DNA (2010), a database had a hit. Matching the killers' (or one of the killers) DNA to some found at the crime scene of my cousin. His name, Alfredo Rolando Prieto, scary-looking guy, as I looked at his picture in the paper, I remember thinking, demon. He looked soul-less.

He had been already sitting on death row first in California, then transferred to Virginia to stand trial for more homicides.' He was found guilty in those cases too and held in Virginia on death row. The murderer actually turned out to be a serial killer. Finally, in 2015 this criminal was to be executed. So while the judicial system and the court protocols and processes of the expected execution were taking place. My family, along with the other family members of ALL the other victims were holding our breaths. Dealing with the undue stress of the back and forth of court. The futile appeals and last-minute attempts, trying to stop the execution from happening. Stacey's mother, Gaylan had suggested everyone wear a blue ribbon during this time.

So my amazing, beautiful, daughter Amanda, had made a box of these pins in support of justice for Stacey. On the lid of the box, it read, 'Grab a Pin for Stacey Lynn.' They were little blue ribbons with a red heart button glued on them. Stacey's favorite color was red. Yes, makes sense, all these memories came flooding back. Just as they are now as I give a thought to them.

Anyways fast forward to current 2021, sitting in my car holding the button this time as I remembered where it came from, a reminder of Stacey was with me, and then stranger still was the thought that crossed my mind-' check the date .' I glanced at my phone and tears began to fall, May 03… Remember when I said in the beginning, I'd tell you the significance of this date. This is the day that Stacey and her boyfriend Tony came up missing. And 2 days later on May 5th, their bodies were found. A wave of an unexplainable mixed emotion flooded over me. I felt like I was floating out of my own body for a moment.

The veil was pulled back and I glimpsed for a moment in amazement, a peace knowing Stacey is with Jesus. He was putting her on my heart with love.

This heart was to *remind* me of her and let me know she is with HIM…

I don't know how many of you think this way, but I do… I believe God loves us so much that He lets the essence of our loved ones stop in on us from time to time. Not that they need us, but rather that we need them. I trust our God knows just what we need and when we need it. I also know- no good thing does He withhold from us. Knowing this, I cry tears of relief, but also feel a bit of grief again for the loss of my cousin. I wonder' why the reminder had to be on this day? This was definitely not a wonderful memory. So, why not allow the little wink, on my cousin's birthday? And then I knew why…

This terrible day of the past connects me with a deeper part of my heart. A part of my heart that is broken and worn (a part that I still *cannot* hide). It's a place that I hold deep in my heart for my cousin. A part which I believe is necessary at times, in order to fully experience the things that are given us spiritually. Connecting our hearts with our spiritual eyes. Keeping us from being devoured by the world. Pulling us *closer to God.*

It's in these moments where we can feel our faith fanned into *flame*.

It's just what we need- Yes- A completely vulnerable, wide-open heart, broken down - no walls, allowing us to soak up those amazing, unexpected moments. Pulling us closer to God and allowing us the spiritual clarity, to view the purposes, for which they were intended. Today this little heart wink gave me the Lord's great- *impenetrable peace* and allowed me to feel a bit of love from my cousin.

Scripture Share

Peace I leave with you; my peace I give to you. Not as the world gives do I give to you. Let not your hearts be troubled, neither let them be afraid.
-(John 14:27. ESV)

Encouragement

No matter what we are doing- even in the monotony of the day, Jesus *is* with us and knows just what we need, even when we ourselves do not. He allows us glimpses …And when we have lost someone special to us, because He is such a good, good God, no goodness does He withhold. So whether you have experienced a reminder of your loved one who has passed by the viewing of a butterfly – hummingbird, ladybug, feather, or even a button. Whatever it is that brings them to mind in connection and closeness to you- as (almost if you sense their essence checking in on you)– It brings us such peace. I believe those moments happen for our benefit and this my friends is just another mysterious gift from God.

As Always in His service -April

✝

In Loving Memory of My Beautiful Cousin
Stacey Lynn Siegrist

He will wipe away every tear from their eyes, and death shall be no more, neither shall there be mourning, nor crying, nor pain anymore, for the former things have passed away."

-*(Revelation 21:4, ESV)*

OBEDIENT BLESSINGS
Darlene Harris

December 11, 2006 –

Leading up to this God-wink moment, I had been in a long season of financial difficulties.

On this particular morning, the cupboards were bare, and I had no money for groceries. For several days with no foreseeable money coming in, I had been praising God for all my past blessings, and in faith, thanking Him for His financial help not yet received. After my prayer time, God's loving voice spoke to me. He said, "Clean out your refrigerator in faith and prepare it for groceries." So I did. I cleaned the entire refrigerator and even cleaned the kitchen cabinets. With a bit of apprehension, I got ready and drove to our post office to get the mail and sure enough, there was an unexpected reimbursement check for $118.00. Even though I was expecting something, I was still stunned at God's mercy and abundant blessing. I went immediately and bought groceries to put in that clean refrigerator and cabinets.

Scripture Share

"Consider this...Whoever offers the sacrifice of thanksgiving glorifies me, and prepares his way so that I will show God's salvation to him."

- (Psalm 50:22-23, WEB)

Encouragement

When you find yourself in dire straits wondering how you're ever going to solve your problem. Encourage yourself in the Lord. Take a few moments and write down all the positive things in your life. Take time to reflect on how God has helped you in the past, Begin thanking Him for all these things, and before long, your faith will increase and you can go to Him with confidence saying, "Thank you, Father, for answering this present need! I give you praise for I know the answer is on its way by faith in Jesus' Powerful Name!"

Blessings-Darlene

DREAM HOME
Denise Thurman

I moved to Los Angeles twenty years ago to pursue an acting and writing career. How's that going, you ask? Well, I am a legal secretary by day -- writer by night. I've had success and obtained some IMDb credits, but somewhere along the way, I became stuck. Stuck in my day job. Stuck in my dreams. Stuck in my growth.

After twenty years I should have been living the dream life in sunny California, right? Let me just say right here and right now, I cried out to God and wasn't getting any clear answers, but what was clear is that my idea of a dream life is not the same as God's. I had a lot of questions. Do I pack up and move home near my family or move somewhere new and exciting and start over again? Can I afford to retire in California? What am I supposed to do, God? I was discouraged, depressed, and felt defeated, but God had a solid infallible plan while I was clueless and crying.

You see, I had been living with a wonderful friend for the past seven years to split expenses. We were so blessed to have our friendship and grow more in Christ during the time we were roommates, which was also part of God's plan!

But I felt like I was just merely existing. I always pictured myself writing amazing scripts in my home office inside my beautiful dream home - someday. The problem - I spent too much time daydreaming and not dream-doing.

We want *change* but we somehow never voluntarily take action to change things.

I felt prompted by God to make a move to a new apartment, but I was still reluctant and nervous about managing my expenses on my own once again and my living situation was working out perfectly as is, so why change it? God was moving me out of my comfort zone because I wouldn't take the initiative myself. And he does that a lot! It was all part of a bigger picture that I didn't see yet. We have to get out of our comfort zones to continue to grow.

In March 2020, I had moved into my new apartment and was feeling more confident that I can do this. Unfortunately, the Coronavirus pandemic had reached a peak and we were quickly given stay-at-home orders. Within the next month, the law firm where I worked began letting employees go and closing down their satellite offices. We eventually took a 10% pay reduction for several months before being reinstated. It was a scary time, but I had to keep reminding myself that God will provide! I held on tight to that in the midst of so much uncertainty. I was so very thankful and grateful to still be employed with a wonderful firm that honestly did the best they could to continue with business as usual (or as close to it as possible).

I worked from home day-in and day-out with little to no physical contact with others in a scary, ever-changing world. I let the pandemic take over my life and I stopped living it. It threw me for a loop. Too much confusion! No answers! I felt like I had circled back to another mid-life crisis. Everything seemed to come to a screeching halt, especially my writing career and my dream home - not to mention my dream husband, but that's another story God's still writing.

Several months had passed and although it was still weird to keep our distance, wash our hands and wear a mask, it started becoming somewhat normal. And then, one night in November of 2020,

I was talking to my friend, and (out of the blue) she mentioned that a home was just listed for sale in her Aunt's community. Why was she telling me this when we're in the middle of a pandemic and when I just moved into a new apartment paying a massive amount of rent with a lease to fulfill. I have no funds to purchase a home after taking a pay reduction for close to five months. But after a back-and-forth Negative Nellie on my part, I thought - why not look? Maybe it will give me ideas and inspire me for my future home. I've done it many times before with homes that were way out of my league.

That weekend, I pulled into a very clean and well-kept mobile home community and parked in front of Space 330. I still had my reservations, and this was not the dream home I had pictured in my mind, until I saw the orange tree in the front yard. As I approached the large front porch to meet the realtor, I saw that it was not just one orange tree, but rather four! And a kumquat tree! Frankly, I really didn't know what kumquats were and had to look them up.

I stepped inside the door to beautiful brand-new flooring, an open dining room with a built-in hutch-type curio cabinet, an open stove area and kitchen bar, laundry room, and guest bath to the side, into a small den, past a second bedroom, and into the back master bedroom and master bath with a gigantic bathtub and a vanity lit up like a Hollywood dressing room. The master bath alone seemed larger than my storage unit I once had. It was an amazing, beautifully remodeled 1,440 square foot home, with a carport and two storage sheds, lush rose bushes out front, and oh, did I mention the orange trees and kumquat tree? Oh, yes, I did. It didn't compare to my small overpriced 800 square foot apartment where my money was floating down the drain.

But I was still not quite sold on it - just that little hesitation of how in the world could I possibly consider this right now? I was thinking this is nice and someday I'll have my dream home that has a vanity like that, or a laundry room like that, or open kitchen and bar area like that or -- maybe an orange tree, or two - or four! And an extra bedroom to turn into my home office to do all that writing that I'm supposed to be doing because that was my dream after all, right? I just needed a *place* to do it! I was drawn to this. I saw so many possibilities for this home. And then I snapped back to reality.

I spoke to the realtor, just curious, how much money are we talking? They had it listed for $129K. That's a bargain for this type of home in southern California, not to mention a safe, quiet, clean neighborhood. My dream home I had in mind was near the half-million mark and stretching further to the million-dollar mark near the beach. But again, my idea of a dream home differs from God's. As I was leaving, the realtor had the duty to remind me that it was a 55+ community and I told him, "I got that covered!" I took it as a compliment.

I left that day with lots of questions and concerns swirling in my head. There's no way I could do this, but it was nice to look. Over the next couple of days, I mulled it over in my brain and prayed so hard. I just couldn't get it out of my head. I was preparing to make an offer just under the asking price when my realtor called and said that someone had already made an offer, so I'd have to go the full asking price. I bit the bullet and did it. Of course, I had to get pre-approved by the bank. My credit is exceptional these days, but would my income be enough? And then, the down payment? All the expenses of home ownership? Unknown territory all around. I had to close my eyes and hold the rail with each step. I closed my eyes to trust God, not myself.

And I grabbed the rail for his steady guidance, not my own path. What was God up to?

Using part of my retirement account was an option. Of course, I would be looking at hefty taxes to pay because I wasn't 59½ yet. But if I look at using my retirement to buy my retirement home, then it made perfect sense and would be paid for by the time I actually retire! I just went with it and prayed - whatever happens God, it happens! I was fine with whatever the outcome.

Then, I received a call from my realtor that there was yet another offer. This was discouraging so I thought of it as a sign that it just wasn't meant to be. My heart was pounding. I was profusely sweating. I just didn't feel comfortable offering more.

There's that word, "feel." Quit *feeling* and start *praying*!

So I prayed. I prayed. I prayed. In that moment I spontaneously opened my Bible to Psalm 131. I *spontaneously* did it, but God *chose* it. I repeated it a few times and what came over me is - things too wonderful for me, content and putting my hope in the Lord now and forevermore.

Psalm 131

> *1 My heart is not proud, Lord,*
> *my eyes are not haughty;*
> *I do not concern myself with great matters*
> *or things too wonderful for me.*
> *2 But I have calmed and quieted myself,*
> *I am like a weaned child with its mother;*
> *like a weaned child I am content.*
> *3 Israel, put your hope in the Lord*
> *both now and forevermore.*

So I called my realtor and told him that I had prayed and read Psalm 131 and firmly gave him the figure of $131. But he quickly said, "131 what?" My heart sank. More heartbeats and more sweat dripping. I was set on that final 131 until my eyes wandered down the page to Psalm 132:5.

My eyes locked in on the number 5, not necessarily the verse, and then I read it…

> *Psalm 132*
>> *1 Lord, remember David*
>> *and all his self-denial.*
>> *2 He swore an oath to the Lord,*
>> *he made a vow to the Mighty One of Jacob:*
>> *3 "I will not enter my house*
>> *or go to my bed,*
>> *4 I will allow no sleep to my eyes*
>> *or slumber to my eyelids,*
>> *5 till I find a **place for the Lord**,...*
>> ***a dwelling** for the **Mighty One of Jacob**."*

A place for the Lord! A dwelling!

You can interpret that any way you want to, but my final response was $131.5, and he quickly said "Congratulations!" The ball was rolling. My mind was reeling. My hands were shaking. My heart was pounding. My eyes were crying. I was sweating. And yet,..

God was winking!

From that moment on (and honestly way before), God was in control. He lined up the perfect realtor, the perfect loan officer, the perfect escrow company, the perfect funds, the perfect timing. It was thirty days of my heart racing through this first-time home-buying process in the middle of a pandemic, but I knew this was directly from God. It may not have been the dream home I had in mind, but it was God's dream home for me on this earth, at this time. And my new neighbors also informed me that there were three other bids and one that even offered cash on the spot. But it came down to God saying, "This is Denise's home." Little ole me! He took care of his child and worked out every detail and more when I had no clue. His gifts are perfect.

I moved into my new home on December 14, 2020, just in time to put up my Christmas tree in a bare living room and an airbed in the bedroom.

I honored my apartment lease until January 15, one month shy of being there a year and paying the additional month while at the same time making my additional house payment. But God provided? Of course, He did! No sweat on His part, but I was sweating profusely as the movers finally placed everything I owned into this new home.

I'm paying less than what I had been paying in rent for a much smaller apartment. I have an investment. I'm in a safe, wonderful neighborhood learning how to take care of the rose bushes, kumquats, and oranges. To come so far from where I was with *no plan*, no hope, and misguided self-direction, God showed up and showed out at a time when I thought it was impossible for me to ever think of buying a home.

So, why didn't I just stay with my roommate until this home was ready? Because moving into my apartment gave me the confidence that I could make it on my own again before he blessed me with such a wonderful gift. Do I worry about the upkeep of my new home? Yes, I'm human, but I know that God will see me through. I'm thankful and blessed beyond measure. He brought me here and He will see me through. God loves me so much! He went ahead of me to lay out the plan and pull me forward to where I was supposed to be. He did all of this behind the scenes when I was crying out to Him for help, for answers - and procrastinating.

I've turned the spare bedroom into my office space where I am writing again and fulfilling the purpose, He has for me in this life, as well as working-from-home as a legal secretary because that still pays the bills.

God can do anything, and nothing alters his plan. I pray that you never miss out on the God-winks! They're all around us...

Scripture Share

Now to him who is able to do immeasurably more than all we ask or imagine, according to his power that is at work within us, to him be glory in the church and in Christ Jesus throughout all generations, forever and ever! Amen.

- (Ephesians 3:20-21, NIV)

Encouragement

I hope you are encouraged by my story. If anything, know that you *can* dream your biggest dream and place it in God's hands. From there, He will turn it into something much bigger than you ever imagined and you will be amazed by His marvelous plan.

Always in His grip-Denise

✝

LAKE SILENCE
Keith Broyles

It was the August of 1973.

I had traveled from Houston with a group of 25 Explorer Scouts to Ely Minnesota for a long canoe trek. Once we arrived in Ely, we flew on "Wilderness Wings Airways," 125 miles into the Canadian forest country and we canoed (and hiked many miles over portage trails carrying the canoes and backpacks) back to the United States.

It was a trip of many firsts for me. Among them, it was my first time to travel that far and long without my parents. That flight on Wilderness Wings was also my first time to fly and it was on a pontoon plane at that. We had been on the trail for almost two weeks. We would cross the border back into the United States the next day. It had been a long two weeks. They were a great bunch of guys but over the course of the trip, since we got off the airplanes, I had seen almost no one but those 25 guys. There are not great numbers of people canoeing through Quetico Provincial Park.

We made camp that last night on a little lake about ten miles north of the border. We all went about our camp responsibilities. We pitched the tents, gathered the firewood, made dinner, and cleaned up after the meal. I don't remember so many years later what my responsibility was that night, I just know I was finished for the night…

I grabbed my canoe paddle and a lifejacket, threw both into the canoe I shared with two other guys, and paddled out to the middle of the lake and sat there watching the sunset. I knew I would hear all about how I knew better than to go out on the water alone (anyone who has ever had experience with Scouts knows you don't do anything on the water without a buddy). I didn't care. I would deal with that later. I was sick of those 24 other guys and needed time alone.

I loved the trip, but I had been away from home most of the summer. I had worked all summer in a job that had me away from home during the week but was home on the weekends.

I immediately followed that up with this canoe trip. I was feeling a bit homesick too. Once I was in the middle of the lake, I sat and watched the sunset. There, the lake lived up to its name, "Silence." No, it wasn't completely silent. could still hear the camp off in the distance, but for me it was quiet…There, in the middle of Lake Silence, for possibly the first time in my life, I felt the presence of God. It wasn't my profession of faith that was a few years before. It wasn't my call to ministry. That was several years away. It was *God* reminding a tired, homesick teenager that he wasn't alone.

Scripture Share

The LORD said, "Go out and stand at the mountain before the LORD. The LORD is passing by." A very strong wind tore through the mountains and broke apart the stones before the LORD. But the LORD wasn't in the wind. After the wind, there was an earthquake. But the LORD wasn't in the earthquake. After the earthquake, there was a fire. But the LORD wasn't in the fire. After the fire, there was a sound. Thin. Quiet. When Elijah heard it, he wrapped his face in his coat. He went out and stood at the cave's entrance. A voice came to him and said, "Why are you here, Elijah?"

- *(1 Kings 19:11-13, CEB)*

Encouragement

We rarely find God in the noise of Life. God is polite and usually will not try to speak over us and the noise we use to fill our ears. It is up to us to seek the time and space where we can hear God speak to us. I used to believe that God was capable of speaking over the noise, and in that much I was right. But God wants us to listen, so God, more often than not, speaks softly.

Filled with His Grace- Keith

AN UNDENIABLE MESSAGE
Nolan Welch

written 05/25/21...

Just a little over a year ago, I was attending one of my best friends' funerals (Brad). He had recently died from a drug overdose while in his car. In this group of friends, there were five of us that were remarkably close.

When I returned home, two days later from the funeral. I walked through the front doors of the rehab I had been staying at, and the first thing I see is two of the five friends together. One was one of the homies, and the other was Brad's girlfriend. They were sitting on the couch hooking up. Mind you Brad had been in the ground for maybe a day. It had really got to me seeing that. So, I grabbed my board and walk straight back out, and skated down to the Santa Monica pier.

I was terribly upset at the site I had just seen. I thought to myself, 'Morals and integrity just do not seem to be in people's values anymore.' Once I got down to the pier, I went to my favorite spot, which is a bench on the end of it. I would normally go there to do my meditation and sit with myself when I was upset, it was my safe space. I remember it being a pretty slow day down there, kind of overcast. I was just sitting there thinking about how life is, how people are, and how I wish I had never witnessed what I had just seen.

Once I was about to leave something told me to try to talk to Brad in my head… (I know it sounds so crazy).

During this time in my life, I was really struggling. I was trying to connect with GOD, however, I decided to try to speak to Brad. I remember just looking up at the sky and thinking "Brad please let me know if anything is out there, I'm really struggling right now man." No joke, not even half a second after I finished that thought, 25 *dolphins* and *sea otters* started popping up out of the water doing like a little dance in front of me.

Not going to lie I started freaking out a little bit and started looking around to see if anyone else was seeing what was going on. Do I think Brad sent that message to me?

I *don't*, I think GOD sent that message to me for Brad just to let me know that he was safe, and it was God showing himself to me through a simple, yet very cool message.

This one girl told me recently that once you let God into your life you will start noticing spiritual messages things meant just for you. Things you would probably never pay attention to if you hadn't let Him in. And I truly believe that was what He was doing. Showing up and letting me know that I am not alone- *He is here.*

Scripture Share

[18] *Open my eyes, that I may behold wondrous things out of your law.*

-(Psalm 119:18, ESV)

---

[18] In Transparency -Nolan never sent me his scripture share, but I considered this verse was fitting. Also if you noticed the verse is Psalm 119:18 and the footnote just happened to be the 18th. It's so wonderfully amazing the ways in which God works all things together.- *love April*

Encouragement

I have struggled for 30 years trying to connect with God. The thing I have learned is that God might not show Himself today, tomorrow, or even the next day, but *don't give up* because when the time is right, I promise He *will* show Himself in a way you would never imagine.

In God we Trust - Nolan

To those who are suffering grief and loss

This next story demonstrates how losing a parent or loved one can change us. How grieving can become a place where we get stuck. Until the day we can open our heart with His help.

As the Lord reaches down touching us, the storm clouds dim and the SON of His love shines on us, allowing us to find closure for the grief that we had carried far too long. To those who are suffering a loss-

Don't quit reaching for Jesus, let Him bring you comfort.
Be thee encouraged ....

> *He heals the brokenhearted*
> *and binds up their wounds.*
> *-(Psalm 147:3, ESV)*

> *"Blessed are those who mourn,*
> *for they shall be comforted.*
> *-(Matthew5,4,ESV)*

MY MENDED HEART
Jacqulynn Brookins

It was September 19th, 2013, that day my heart felt numb, that day I lost my precious rose!

I place it in my heart, I thought that it would be there protected forever , I loved it. The day that I lost my mother was unreal, so unbelievable. I could not believe it…My rose withered, my mom passed away before I could get to her side, my only thought was Mom I am coming. I am on my way.

You see it was my birthday the next month October 28th, but she couldn't wait.

(Mom, I miss you so much! The pain of you not being here anymore overwhelms me. Trying to breathe to take in air burns my chest, you were my everything. I tried to accept it, to believe that it was real, it was true.)

We buried her September 28, 2013.

She was beautifully dressed, her hair, her face but she wasn't there. Leaving her on the east coast while I travel back to the west coast in a state of disbelief, it was as if I just had just visited. My mind never letting me believe in the unbelievable.

This feeling of loss- I carry it in my heart like a child in my arms, I nurtured it. Her favorite words " Let Go and let God "; her song " Walk Around Heaven All Day ", One of these Mornings.

[19]It was her love for the Lord that helped carry me through.

It was even the simplest things I missed. The way she would say, "Yes." The way she would call my name! She loved me, miles apart we were. She was on the East Coast and me the West Coast. She hating earthquakes and I hating tornados, so we stayed parted. I mourned her. Not to hear her voice ever again was inconceivable… How can I see "Rest In Peace" for her? When I had not accepted that she was gone ; I will always miss her.

---

[19] **Proverbs 22:6 KJV-[6]** *Train up a child in the way he should go: and when he is old, he will not depart from it.*

I didn't get to kiss her lips, feel the warmth of her face before she left, I wanted her with me. At her age, a change would have been too much, so I watched her board the airplane wondering ; When will I see her again. I wanted her with me, but the doctors said not to force her to stay. I watched her go to a home other than my own, back to the East Coast. I allowed my mind to rest as she returned home, back to other loved ones.

Now as I go on, I looked back with a heavy heart knowing that she did not just leave me her baby girl. This year 2022, I take each day! Just breathing; Mom! This year I needed her if it was just only to hear her voice ! I needed my MOM. She is on my heart!

I still cry when I think of you Mrs. Dorothy Mae Lee Edwards, you were my mother.

When people post about your death I never said or posted anything words; no pictures I asked myself why? BECAUSE I DID *NOT* REGISTER HER DEATH, I still felt dazed of it. I had no desire to go among the saints, to be comforted, to be told those words about her being gone.

Even though I remember telling Father it's okay I didn't want her to suffer, but "I DID NOT GET TO SEE HER, NO ...WHY? You had a reason, this is what I had to accept, I had to accept. So I made a place in my prayer garden for her where I can go and have a little talk with her in the Prescence of the Lord.
Mother's Day is here. My Mom would always say 'LET GO AND LET GOD'!

...So I begin to read scriptures;

Proverbs 16:9, *A man's heart deviseth his way; but the Lord directeth his steps*! Isaiah 26;3, *Thou wilt keep him in perfect peace, whose mind is stayed on thee: because he trusteth in thee.* Roman 8:28 *And we know that all things work together for good to them that love God to them who are the called according to his purpose.* Lord As in Proverbs 16:9-*you know my heart*, in Isaiah 26:3 *you give me perfect peace*, in Roman 8:28, *you have a calling for me.*

I *have* a purpose.

On May 7th, the day before Mother's Day I became so emotional, crying every day. I had decided to go back to *church*, I had refused to go. I was angry with myself because my mother was still in my heart; I had placed her there so close. Now she is gone on MOTHERS DAY, It is time...

I grieve her for the last time, now is time for great memories filled with love. Death will become us all one day.

Mom I love you…

Encouragement

I will have no more pain or suffering when I remember her. I will remember her smile, always. On this day, Oh this glorious day, I would love to give praises and honor to our Father God, our Lord and Savior Jesus Christ. Who in His time as we stay soaked in His word will help us in our afflictions, bring comfort to our grieving hearts and bind up our wounds….

A Mended Heart- Jacqulynn

✝

In Loving Memory of
Mrs. Dorothy Mae Lee Edwards

Jacqulynn and her mom

As one whom his mother comforts, so I will comfort you; you shall be comforted in Jerusalem.

-(Isaiah 66:13 ESV)

EPILOGUE

The idea for this book series came to me by Divine inspiration. The stories in it and the order they were written and shared, all appointed by the Lord. He guided my steps every bit of the way. I am eternally grateful to Jesus for such a wonderful fulfilling purpose. I pray to continue these books, well, until HE says, I no longer can.

I hope you have been blessed by these beautiful true experiences, that were so bravely shared. And I pray that you feel that much closer to our beautiful Lord Jesus. Remember no matter what your going through…

Jesus is with *you*.

Right there, wherever you are.
You are not alone.
And most importantly
You are **forgiven** and **loved**, *unconditionally*.

OTHER GOOD WORKS CONTRIBUTORS PAGE

April Yarber/ Compiler / Contributor
FROM FLICKER TO FLAME SERIES DEVELOPER
Speakingtothehearts@gmail.com
Author, *Speaking to the Heart Moments with Jesus- daily devotional*
Trilogy Publishing 2019

Rev. J. Keith Broyles, D.Min./ Contributor
LAKE SILENCE
Pastor, Perritte Memorial United Methodist Church
Nacogdoches, TX
Author, *Average Joe: With an Extraordinary Story*
Amazon Direct Publishing 2019

Jackie Gebbia/ Contributor
HE LIVES,
THE WHITE FEATHER
HE HEARS YOU
Screenwriter, Graphic Designer
Occupy Culture Founder 2021, occupycultureinfo@gmail.com

Denise Thurman/ Contributor
MY DREAM HOME
Screenwriter, Author, *Heaven won't be Heaven without You*, Author house 2013

OTHER GOOD WORKS CONTRIBUTORS PAGE

Darlene Harris/ Contributor
OBEDIENT BLESSINGS
Blog Author, *Rooms filled with Treasures*
Website www.roomsfilledwithtreasures.com
Author, *Stepping Stone to a Better Life* *2018*; available on the website for free downloads

Priscilla James Cruz/ Contributor
THE VISION
Co- Founder, *Western Monarch Guardians*
Orange County, California *1998*
Educator, helping to save the Monarch Butterflies
Facebook page: Monarch Guardians

James R Berg/ Contributor
FOCUS ON HIM
Owner Operator, *Crystal Waters Pool, and Spa*
Orange County, California

Amanda Turney/ Cover designer
BOOK COVER GRAPHIC DESIGN
Hair Stylist, Orange County, California

'Speaking to the Heart From Flicker to Flame Book Series'

Volume One

Moments beyond the Veil

'Speaking to the Heart From Flicker to Flame Book Series'

An on-going series of True Faith Experiences...

If you have a true faith story, you would like to contribute for consideration and possible publication in a future volume- please email

at

Speakingtothehearts@gmail.com

For more check out my author page on Amazon
https://www.amazon.com/author/aprilyarber

If you need prayer or would like to pray for others please come join my Facebook group faith family at:

With love April Amanda and Autumn

And *Don't forget* if you enjoyed this book- Please Kindly Review

My goal is to reach as many people as I can with the hope and love of Jesus

Reviews will help us reach more hearts,
Thank you from my heart to yours!

Always in His Service

April

Heart Notes

Heart Notes

www.ingramcontent.com/pod-product-compliance
Lightning Source LLC
Chambersburg PA
CBHW021102080526
44587CB00010B/341